Philosophy of Existence

Works in Continental Philosophy

GENERAL EDITOR JOHN R. SILBER

 Karl Jaspers

PHILOSOPHY
OF
EXISTENCE

Translated and with an Introduction
by Richard F. Grabau

PHILADELPHIA

University of Pennsylvania Press

Originally published by Walter de Gruyter & Co.,
Berlin, under the title *Existenzphilosophie,* Third
Edition copyright by Walter de Gruyter & Co.

Copyright © 1971 in the English translation by the
Trustees of the University of Pennsylvania. English
translation by Richard F. Grabau.
Library of Congress Catalog Card Number:
79-133203

ISBN: 0-8122-7629-9 (Cloth)
ISBN: 0-8122-1010-7 (Paper)

Seventh printing, 1995

MANUFACTURED IN THE UNITED STATES OF AMERICA

Editor's Note

Philosophy of Existence by Karl Jaspers was first presented to the public thirty years ago as a series of lectures invited by The German Academy of Frankfurt. In preparing these lectures Jaspers, whom the Nazis had already dismissed from his professorship at Heidelberg, knew he was speaking in Germany for the last time—unless and until National Socialism were annihilated. Resisting temptations to easy and ineffectual martyrdom and silence, Jaspers used the occasion to offer an account of the cultural and intellectual situation from which existentialism emerged as well as a summary of his own philosophy. "In this total threat," Jaspers writes, "I tried to pay homage to reason, to be bound to the sciences, to become aware of what was essential, and to think in the ground of all being." In so doing Jaspers prepared lectures that spoke directly and tellingly to his hearers. And because he did not allow the historical events of 1937 to determine the contents of his lectures, they also speak with undiminished directness and force to us.

Philosophy of Existence serves three purposes today; it brings the many strands of the existential movement into focus; it provides an excellent overview of Jaspers' own philosophical position, which is becoming increasingly available to English and American readers as more of his books are translated; and it demonstrates by example that philosophy need not be irrational, anti-scientific, journalistic, or homiletic in order to be existential and *engagé*.

In this short book Jaspers, one of our leading existentialist philosophers, provides a much needed corrective for the popular view of existentialism as a pessimistic, irrationalist philosophy. Jaspers maintains that it is, rather, part of the mainstream of Western philosophy—the form that philosophy has taken in our day. Since Socrates proclaimed the virtue of the examined life, the task of philosophy has been to give a reflective account of human existence, to clarify and illuminate human life. It has done this both by critical inquiries into many areas of human experience, and by constructing ontological accounts of reality. In the former effort philosophy has developed such specialties as logic, ethics, epistemology, philosophies of religion, science, mind, value, art, and so forth. In the latter it has attempted to draw its results into a vision of the totality of being. Jaspers continues this two-fold philosophical task by rational and critical methods. He insists that philosophy cannot be irrational since its only tool is reason and that it cannot be the expression of a merely subjective and particular viewpoint since it must be intelligible and communicable to others.

But philosophy must be concerned with man in his concrete physical, historical, social, and personal situation. It cannot or should not reduce human existence to one or even several of its dimensions. Jaspers argues that in the nineteenth and twentieth centuries this is precisely what philosophy has done: it has departed from its vital aim and tried to imitate rather than clarify or explain the sciences. It has theorized about man as though he were an object in the world like other things, an object to be understood by the same kind of detached and objective investigation. Existentialism is a reaction against pseudoscientific philosophizing, and the term "existential" (Existenz) focuses this reaction by calling our attention to the concrete human situation from which philosophical thought arises.

The two philosophers from whom Jaspers has learned the most are Kierkegaard and Kant. From the former comes Jaspers' sensitivity to man's concreteness and individuality. From the latter comes Jaspers' respect for science, his method, and his view of reason as the principle of both criticism and unity. These influences are woven by Jaspers into an account of science, religion, metaphysics, knowledge and truth—an account which tries to do justice to the concreteness, individuality, and finitude of human existence. The result is a philosophy that is critical and rational while also open to the possibilities, inscrutabilities, and freedom of human life.

Philosophy of Existence, I believe, is the finest introduction to Jaspers' own comprehensive philosophy and to existentialism as a philosophical movement.

JOHN R. SILBER

Austin, Texas
August, 1970

Contents

Preface

IN THIS LITTLE BOOK Karl Jaspers provides one of the best short statements of both the main features of his own philosophy and his ideas about the nature and importance of philosophical thought in human life. Since he had just been dismissed from his university position by the Nazis, the lectures of 1937 which gave rise to this volume were his last opportunity for public statement for several years. They were delivered six years after the appearance of his *Philosophie*.* Although his gigantic *Von der Wahrheit* (*On Truth*) was not to be published for ten years (and is still not available in English), most of it was already written and the content of the present book was taken from it. As a result, these three lectures by Jaspers contain all his major ideas: the encompassing, existential truth, exception and authority, transcendence and transcending thought, reason, metaphysics and cipher language, and the relation between philosophy and its two closest styles of thought which are science and religion.

* Philosophy, *3 vols; E. B. Ashton, trans., University of Chicago Press, 1969–1971.*

According to Jaspers, existential philosophy is neither new nor radically different from what usually goes by the name of philosophy. Straight off in the introductory lecture he insists that it is an integral part of what he calls the "one, primordial philosophy." The only thing new about it is that at present Existenz is the key term. One understands Jaspers, then, only by understanding his conception of philosophical thought and the role played by Existenz as the concept around which all others are clustered and organized. These two ideas are not separate. Philosophy derives its unique features from the fact that it is performed by man as Existenz.

Philosophy, Science and Religion. Jaspers hardly ever speaks of 'philosophy.' Instead, he prefers to use the present infinitive of the verb '*philosophieren,*' which I have translated as 'philosophizing.' By using this term Jaspers stresses the fact that philosophy is an activity, a movement of thought that knows no end and produces no set of doctrines, theories, or even concepts. Philosophizing is a process of thinking as inner action in which the thinker comes to an authentic awareness of himself and reality by pressing beyond or transcending everything objective. From the standpoint of the subjectivity of the thinker philosophizing can be described as the elucidation or clarification of Existenz. From the standpoint of the objects it is concerned with, philosophizing is the expression of an encounter with (intrinsic) being. This expression takes two directions: a reflection on the nature and limits of objective knowledge, which Jaspers calls world orientation, and a transcending thinking in which being itself comes to expression, which he calls metaphysics.

Philosophy is not only unable to provide objective theories; it also depends upon and lives at the boundaries of other disciplines. Philosophical understanding consists in part of an appreciation of the difference between philosophy and these other disciplines. In Jaspers' view the two most central to philosophy are science and religion, which are in fact the sources from which philosophizing springs.

Science is essential to philosophy. Without knowledge of science a philosopher has no knowledge of the world. He is, practically, blind. It is no accident that throughout history the greatest philosophers have been familiar with science. Unless it incorporates the scientific method as well as its results, philosophizing becomes mere speculation, reverie, or perhaps the expression of subjective vital interests or desires. Furthermore, Jaspers agrees with the positivists that questions of knowledge and fact are all scientific questions. Only through science do we learn to know the way things are. For this reason philosophy cannot produce any theories of its own. When it tries to become a science by claiming knowledge in its own right, it cuts a ridiculous figure.

If philosophy is not science, neither is science philosophy. Science is a process of thought involving precise and publicly verifiable concepts and methods. It views reality in terms of these constructions. Hence, it has definite limits. When reality is identified with what science alone can know, science itself becomes superstition. It becomes a narrow and unfounded philosophical position which turns everything, including man, into an object. Both being and human existence lose their depth. Philosophizing has the task of pointing out the nature of science and the limits of its application. In doing this, philosophy transcends science and gives evidence of another source from which philosophizing springs. Jaspers calls this source transcendence. One becomes aware of transcendence in the process of thinking beyond the limits of scientific knowledge. In this way Jaspers comes to the realization that both the thinker and reality are more than what can be known about them in objective terms. No known object is being itself.

Although Jaspers often claims that science is essential to philosophy, it is also true that the methods and doctrines of science do not enter into the content of his philosophy in any interesting or significant ways, as they do in Descartes, Leibnitz or Kant. Knowledge of science, according to Jaspers, keeps a philosopher from claiming to have factual and objective knowledge. But beyond this, there is little that science, either by its method or its results, contributes to philosophy. One must know science, it seems, in order to learn how not to philosophize.

Religion is the other source from which philosophizing springs. Through religion men have always given expression both to their own transcendence and to the transcendence of being beyond the natural world. Reality is more than our objective knowledge reveals; it transcends all the immanent levels of conceptual thought, which, in turn, may be viewed as appearances of this transcendence. Man, conceived in religious terms, is also more than a natural being. He is more than his objective knowledge conceives him to be. Because it considers man in relation to God and beyond all the conceptions and exigencies of life, thought and society, religion preserves man's transcendence, dignity and freedom. For this reason, philosophizing affirms religion and sees in it a source of its own idea of transcendence. Without the sense of the transcendence of being conveyed by religion, philosophy itself withers and dies. Reality, collapsing into its immanent modes, consists only of determinate natural objects acting in accordance with objective laws.

Even though philosophy is closely attached to religion, there is a sense in which it is as much opposed to religion as it is to absolutizing science. The chief defect of religion lies in its habit of objectifying transcendence in particularistic symbols which are claimed to be authoritative for all men. Each religion recognizes as adequate only its own representation of transcendence; it sets forth one ideal of humanity, one set of truths and rules for action, to which all men must conform. In this process of objectifying what lies beyond all objectivity, religion destroys human freedom and transcendence just as science does when its objective conceptions of reality are absolutized into a philosophical dogma.

Philosophy, then, is different from both science and religion and yet it is bound to both. From science it gains critical, factual and objective knowledge. From religion it receives the idea of transcendence, although in a determinate and hence unacceptable form. In the process of coming to an awareness of the human situation and its authentic possibilities, however, philosophy must point out the defects and limits of both disciplines. Living thus at the boundaries of knowledge and religious faith, philosophy grasps the truth of being itself lying beyond those boundaries but coming to expression only within them.

The Encompassing. The basic idea in Jaspers' philosophy is that of the encompassing (*das Umgreifende*). It is Jaspers' name for the form of our awareness of being which underlies all our scientific and common-sense knowledge and which is given expression in the myths and rituals of religion. But it can never become an object. Awareness of the encompassing is achieved by reflection upon our situation. As we reflect, we realize that all objects we are aware of, including religious ones, are determinate beings situated in a larger, encompassing context or horizon. We can enlarge the extent of our knowledge, but we can never escape the fact that it is fragmentary and only indefinitely extendable. It has limits. We are always within a horizon. The realization that we cannot make the whole of reality into an object *is* our awareness of the encompassing horizon of being in which all objects of awareness appear. Thus, the encompassing is a term that does not refer to any particular thing. Instead, it expresses a felt quality of all our experience and thought.

Jaspers discusses the encompassing in terms of what he calls its 'modes.' To see what these are and how he derives them, one must understand something about his intentional view of consciousness. According to this view, consciousness is always awareness *of* something. Every act of awareness is therefore analyzable according to a model in which a subject is related to an object. The relationship may be of many kinds: sensory awareness, conceptual thought, feeling, emotion, action, and so on, each susceptible to an indefinite number of possible variations. The general relation of subject to object, therefore, is the horizon or encompassing background of all awareness, and the particular ways that a subject may be related to an object can be called modes of this encompassing. The analysis of the encompassing is thus an elucidation of the main ways a subject is related to an object. Because this subject-object relation is the basic model, the main modes of the encompassing are two: the encompassing that we are (the subject) and the encompassing that being itself is (the object). An analysis of subjectivity provides Jaspers with three main divisions of these modes: existence (*Dasein*), consciousness-in-general, and spirit. We shall return to these presently.

In addition, corresponding to the scientific-immanent and religious-transcendent levels of awareness, Jaspers identifies two other basic divisions of the encompassing. Remembering that the general structure is that of the subject-object relation, we get a transcendent mode of subjectivity (Existenz) and of objectivity (Transcendence.)

We can represent Jaspers' analysis of the encompassing in the following diagram:

THE ENCOMPASSING

The Encompassing of Subjectivity	*The Encompassing of Objectivity*
A. Immanent modes. Existence Consciousness in general Spirit	A. Immanent mode World
B. Transcendent Mode Existenz	B. Transcendent Mode Transcendence.

The idea of the encompassing is complicated by the fact that each of its modes is also an encompassing, that is, an infinite and inexhaustible dimension. Within each of these levels we must distinguish between determinate subject-object relations and the indefinite background of possible relations. For example, at the level of existence men establish particular techniques for interacting with each other and with their environment in order to satisfy their desires and interests. But existence is not exhausted by a description of these techniques. It transcends them, for it is a creative source of new techniques. The same is true of all the other modes. Hence, at each level we never succeed in completely reducing the encompassing to a definitive set of objective relations between subjects and objects. There is always the possibility of further or different determinations of these relations. This implies that even in the immanent modes, where being and man are amenable to objective, scientific investigation, both man and being transcend what can be known about them.

There are three immanent modes of the subject-object relationship, their names deriving, as stated previously, from the subject side of the relation. Man is first an organic being who is there, who exists in a practical life-world in space and time. He has instincts, needs, and drives; he acts so as to satisfy them. The objects he is related to at this level are the objects of his practical concern and they constitute the world of ordinary experience. Jaspers calls this mode "*Dasein.*" Wherever Jaspers uses the term "*Dasein,*" I have translated it by the English word "existence," because *Dasein* is the ordinary German word for existence. Some translators have used "being-there," pointing out that it is a transliteration of *Da-sein.* But "being-there" is not an ordinary English word; it has the aura of a technical term, which in Jaspers it is not. Earle translated it as "empirical existence" in *Reason and Existenz.* This practice raises expectations of another kind of existence—perhaps nonempirical existence—which again is not the case for Jaspers. Besides, Jaspers generally uses the word without any adjectives.

Jaspers' use of *Dasein* must also be distinguished from Heidegger's. In *Being and Time,* Heidegger *does* use *Dasein* as a technical term. It is the name for human existence and is defined by Heidegger's existential categories such as care, freedom, historicity, fallenness, and so forth. Hence, it includes what Jaspers uses two words to express: existence in the ordinary sense and *Existenz,* which *is* a technical term in Jaspers' philosophy and which will be explained presently.

The second immanent mode of subjectivity is consciousness in general, or abstract rational and conceptual understanding. The world man knows at this level is not the world of ordinary experience. It is the world as represented in the sciences. The concepts and method employed by consciousness in general are public and verifiable, and its knowledge is universal and objective. This abstract level is common to all men, and is unique to no one. Hence, Jaspers says that at this level men are point-consciousnesses and interchangeable units.

The third immanent level is spirit. Borrowing the term from Hegel and the subsequent German idealist tradition, Jaspers often talks of spirit as a kind of synthesis of existence and abstract consciousness in general. Like existence, it is concrete and historical. Like consciousness in general, it is universal. It is, then, a concrete universal which Jaspers calls "idea." As men participate in this concrete universal, they are bound together into historic unities. Examples of such unities are: the nation, a church or religion, a cultural tradition, professional organizations, etc. Each of these is formed by an idea. When viewed under the idea of spirit, men are not considered as individuals, but as members of totalities. One can get a sense of the objective pole of this level by reflecting on the 'worlds' of politics, art, or science.

Existence, consciousness in general, and spirit—and the worlds corresponding to them—comprise the immanent modes of the encompassing. But they do not exhaust it. There are in addition the transcendent modes of *Existenz* and Transcendence. The centrality of these two modes, and especially of *Existenz,* constitutes the distinctive character of contemporary existential philosophy as the present form of the perennial philosophy. Emphasis upon them is a protest against the objectifying and dehumanizing tendencies in modern thought (philosophical as well as scientific) and against our increasingly technological and rationalized culture. The nature of these two modes and the relation between them are not very clear. But the following interpretation comes close to what Jaspers intends.

Existenz cannot be described even in a general way as the immanent modes can. Because it is a possibility in all men, it can only be pointed to or appealed to. But two features of it stand out. First, it is absolutely unique. It is each individual human being as a particular, concrete historical being in so far as he is authentic. In this sense Jaspers uses *Existenz* to refer to individual persons. He speaks of *Existenz* as doing or willing something. Secondly, Existenz is the ultimate source or ground of each individual self. In this latter capacity, it is best thought of as a principle of freedom, creativity, or pure spontaneity. It does not refer to an individual, but to a quality of life—authentic existence—in which individuals may or may not participate. In this sense *Existenz* is a universal structure, and Jaspers describes it by means of such concepts as historicity, freedom, resoluteness, and so on. In addition, he almost always refers to it as "possible *Existenz*" rather than as an actuality, because in principle it can never be fully actualized. Every actualization of *Existenz* results in some concrete and determinate creation, that is, some objectification of itself. But *Existenz* remains an origin (*Ursprung*), a limitless field of possibility. Consequently, man as *Existenz* completely transcends all that he is, knows or does. *Existenz* is the primordial, spontaneous depth of each self. Never given, it must be actualized by each person.

Yet there are no direct or immediate manifestations of *Existenz*. All knowledge and action must occur in the world in one or more of the three immanent modes. So *Existenz* seems to be a principle of spontaneity or creativity within *them*. It is man as *Existenz* who continually breaks out of established patterns to create new historical organizations at the level of existence, new knowledge and understanding at the level of consciousness in general, and new ideas in the realm of the spirit, as in morals, art, religion.

In view of these considerations, one can see that "*Existenz*" is a technical term in Jaspers' philosophy. It acquires its meaning from the ways Jaspers uses it and the things he says about it. Because the ordinary English word "existence" would be a misleading translation of *Existenz,* I have incorporated this German term in the translation and have treated it as an English word.

Corresponding to Existenz is transcendence. Transcendence is the representation of being itself beyond all objectivity. The world is an immanent reflection of it. Thus, transcendence expresses the dual feature that within any level of the world one never fully articulates all possibilities, and that beyond objective determination is a background or horizon of being itself to which Existenz is related. Because transcendence is being-itself, Jaspers says that Existenz is aware of itself as given to itself by transcendence. If there were no transcendence, if the world were all there were to being, Existenz would not be possible. Man would be a mundane being, describable in the concepts of the various immanent modes of the encompassing.

A sense of Existenz and transcendence develops in our experience of the great philosophers, artists and scientists. In their systems of thought and representations one senses something more than thought, some source of which their creations are symbols or, as Jaspers says, ciphers. Everything and anything can be a cipher of transcendence. It has only to be viewed in the correct way, and the correct way is from the viewpoint of Existenz and its freedom.

Neither Existenz nor transcendence are objects. They are sources from which everything else springs. But to talk about them is to bring them within the domain of consciousness and its subject-object structure. By necessity, then, we make objects out of them. Hence, talking about them is always liable to misunderstanding: One may take the propositions in their literal sense rather than as pointing to the indeterminate source. One may claim to have objective knowledge about man and being.

But what Jaspers is aiming at is an inner awareness of Existenz and its relation to transcendence. Consequently, one must read Jaspers in such a way as to perform the inner action of transcending thought along with him. Until one takes his sentences and concepts as *signa,* or pointers, Jaspers' philosophy evades him. Only when it is appropriated inwardly by the reader does it take on its full meaning and become free of misunderstanding which itself is a cipher of transcendence.

Despite the hazard of misunderstanding, one can try to get a grip on Jaspers' philosophy by describing it in terms of traditional classifications. So considered, Jaspers comes out an idealist. Many themes in his philosophizing, but especially the clarification of the immanent modes of the encompassing, suggest the idealist stance. Jaspers lumps the objective pole into one entity called world, but he carefully distinguishes between existence, consciousness in general, and spirit. It is evident that there are world-counterparts to each of these subjective modes. But it is also evident that all the energy and priority is put into the subjective mode. Even transcendence *is* only for Existenz. And, although Jaspers says that transcendence is basic and ultimate, the source of Existenz, all his analyses show that what he says about transcendence is derived from the uniqueness and freedom of Existenz. Jaspers is therefore an 'existential' idealist.

Truth and Reality. The last two lectures deal with truth and reality. Both concepts must be viewed against the background of the encompassing and its modes with especial attention to Existenz and transcendence. Here only a few points can be made:

1. Truth is not a simple idea. For Jaspers the term 'truth' has a special meaning within each mode of the encompassing. At the level of existence truth is what works, what leads to the satisfaction of our vital needs and in-

terests. For consciousness in general truth is a function of rational tests and methods, and is universal and compelling for all. At the level of spirit the truth of an idea is its power to establish and to secure spiritual totalities. Finally, the truth of Existenz is unique, particular and historic. It makes no claim at all to universality and objectivity, but because it is the basis of Existenz, the truth by which one lives, so to speak, it is absolute for the Existenz who accepts it. Here truth is a function of faith or commitment. It is Kierkegaard's idea of truth as subjectivity.

2. In spite of the fragmentation of truth into the truths within the modes of the encompassing and the truth of Existenz into the pluralities of Existenzen, there is a sense in which truth is one: the truth of being itself. But this one truth is only an ideal; it is never realized. Jaspers sees each authentic truth at the other levels as a symbol which points to the one truth which binds everything together and which yet is inaccessible, for every actual truth is an historic achievement in a concrete situation. Moreover, the truth of Existenz springs from the freedom and creativity of each Existenz. For Jaspers the one truth of being remains a matter of existential faith which he takes to be the presupposition of all thought and action. But since nothing definite is or can be said about this truth, it remains, for the most part, an organic part of Jaspers' own philosophical commitment. Whether it is only this, or, as Jaspers insists, necessary to philosophy is a question the reader may try to answer as he reads and reflects.

3. Corresponding to the subject-object structure of awareness, especially in the relation between Existenz and transcendence, are forms of truth which Jaspers calls *exception* and *authority*. He takes these terms from Kierkegaard. The truth of each primordial, free and

creative Existenz is an exception in relation to universal truth. No universal truth or historical tradition encloses Existenz. It breaks out of all objectivities and demands the right to establish its own truth creatively. One is reminded of Nietzsche's superman transvaluing all given values and truths and establishing values and truths of his own as he comes to realize his creative possibilities— or of Kierkegaard's knight of faith, whose relation to the absolute allows him to suspend the judgments of objective ethics. The exception demands recognition as an exception, not on the basis of any arbitrary will-to-power, but in the interest of the truth of transcendence which evades objectification even while it permeates all the other modes. The exception is thus the servant of transcendence, or, as Jaspers says, the universal. His very life is testimony to the finite and limited character of all knowledge and practical arrangements. He preserves the freedom of man and the transcendence of being in his exceptional status.

If the exception exhausted the idea of truth, there would be a danger of its degenerating into mere willfulness. So Jaspers pairs it with another form of truth which he calls *authority*. Authority is based upon transcendence. Because all appearances at all the modes of the encompassing are symbols of transcendence, they have authority for men. An example of authority is the cultural tradition in which every person lives and matures. Without this tradition he would be nothing but an aggregate of purely biological and psychological drives. His tradition gives him substance and form—in short his *human* being. But at the same time this tradition is limited; it is historical, partial and only one among many traditions. It contains possibilities which Existenz is free to realize and tendencies it must resist. But when the exception resists authority, it should be done in a spirit of fear and trem-

bling (to use Kierkegaard's terms) or in a spirit of serious-
ness and respect for authority (after the manner of
Socrates in the *Apology* and *Crito*). There is no final
resolution of the opposition between exception and authority. Creative life itself is the dialectical process of
their interplay and history is the outcome of this interplay. Because the creative process is performed by concrete Existenzen, its results can not be foreseen, nor can
techniques be developed to control it.

4. Jaspers develops a concept of reason at the end of
the lecture on truth. Following Kant, he carefully distinguishes reason from the understanding. The latter, it
turns out, is precisely identical with consciousness-in-
general. The domain of the understanding is the domain
of objective, scientific, compelling knowledge. It is
directed towards determinate objects and thinks about
them discursively in terms of testable concepts.

Reason, on the other hand, seems to be a motive within
Existenz. Jaspers speaks of it as will—a will to unity and
a will to communication. Reason not only respects but
actively seeks out what is foreign to it in order to communicate with it and to project an encompassing unity
which includes everything and lets nothing sink into
oblivion. It seeks to go beyond all limits, all separations,
all animosities, to present a total picture of being itself.
But there is no total picture. There is no way of subsum-
ing all the modes of the encompassing, all historical
periods and traditions, all Existenzen and their particular
truths and values into one harmonious whole. There is
only the will to communicate with everyone and everything; there is only the spirit of honesty and openness.
There is only a posture of reason, or an atmosphere of
reason, based upon a faith in transcendence and the unity
of all things in it. Reason is the basis of Jaspers' doctrine
of the encompassing. As a frame of mind or existential

attitude which is aware of the horizonal character of all our thought and action, it continually upsets the putatively complete pictures and theories that claim to be adequate analyses of all reality and presses on to further unity. It is a vision of the one transcendent reality beyond all finite interpretation that emerges from the self-awareness of Existenz in the presence of transcendence. Throughout history reason has been most adequately manifested in philosophy, which Jaspers calls "one great hymn to reason." But by making claims to absolute truth, philosophy has also corrupted reason into an intellectual grasp of objects. For Jaspers everything depends upon our preserving the sense of reason as a radical openness, a binding force and a total will to communication.

5. The final point to note is Jaspers' idea of reality, with which he deals in his last lecture. As he uses the term, reality is identical with being-itself beyond all its finite appearances. He develops the concept by means of three examples. Reality is being beyond all possibility, it is historicity and it is unity. Reality so conceived is reached by an act of transcending thought (reason) in which one leaps out of the realm of the finite and stands before being itself. Only in this union is there any final rest and peace.

In one sense, of course, there is no union with being, pure and simple. Jaspers is not a mystic. Access to being can be had only through the world. Only as one participates in the levels of existence, consciousness in general and spirit in an attitude of reason, can one interpret his historical situation and his daily task as appearances of being, his acts of knowing as revelations of being, and his spiritual creations as its symbols. All these things become ciphers of ultimate reality which must be interpreted by each Existenz. Although nothing is a cipher by any natural right or special property, everything can be seen as a cipher pointing to being itself. Philosophizing is the process of allowing all things to open themselves to being and become its symbols.

Reality can be grasped only historically in terms of particular symbols. Hence there can be no adequate interpretation of it. Unlike religion, which makes transcendence into a supernatural determinate object, philosophizing brings all things into the domain of reason and regards them as transparent ciphers pointing to being. Because in philosophizing each individual recognizes his own truth as a mere cipher, he is able to recognize and respect the truths of other Existenzen and historical traditions. They are ciphers, also. Everything is united in the One. When this state of mind is reached, an attitude emerges which Jaspers in another place calls absolute consciousness. Here, in the vision which perceives being in all finite things, the quest finds an ultimate rest. One senses that being is and stands silent before the ultimate mystery.

With the mention of reason and reality and the contrast with religion and its objectifying view, we are back at our starting point. Now perhaps we can see what Jaspers means by calling philosophy a process of philosophizing, an inner action whose result is not knowledge of any object, or a theory about objects, but a vision of authentic reality in its symbolic appearances. This vision is at the same time an awareness of one's own authentic being. This attitude of mind and thought which transcends everything finite and objective, allowing being itself to reveal itself in its appearances, is what Jaspers means by the perennial philosophy. It has taken many forms, but today, because of the objectifying tendency in modern thought and culture, this philosophy must become an existential philosophy.

RICHARD F. GRABAU

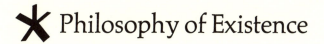 Philosophy of Existence

Introduction

I HAVE been invited to speak about the philosophy of existence.[1] Part of philosophy today goes by this name. The distinguishing term "existence" is meant to emphasize that it is of the present.

What is called philosophy of existence is really only a form of the one, primordial philosophy. It is no accident, however, that for the moment the word "existence" became the distinguishing term. It emphasized the task of philosophy that for a time had been almost forgotten: *to catch sight of reality at its origin and to grasp it through the way in which I, in thought, deal with myself—in inner action.* From mere knowledge of something, from ways of speaking, from conventions and role-playing—from all kinds of foreground phenomena—philosophizing wanted to find its way back to reality. *Existenz* is one of the words for reality, with the accent Kierkegaard gave it: everything essentially real is for me only by virtue of the fact

1. *Throughout this book "philosophy of existence" is a translation of "Existenzphilosophie," "existence" the translation of "Dasein," and "Existenz," where it occurs alone, is left untranslated. For an explanation of these practices, see the Preface, p. xxi.*

that I am I myself. We do not merely exist; rather, our existence is entrusted to us as the arena and the body for the realization of our origin.

Already in the nineteenth century, movements with this turn of mind kept recurring. People wanted "life," wanted "really to live." They demanded "realism." Instead of wanting merely to know, they wanted to experience for themselves. Everywhere, they wanted the "genuine," searched for "origins," and wanted to press on to *man* himself. Superior men became more clearly visible; at the same time, it became possible to discover the true and the real in the smallest particle.

If for a century now the tenor of the age has been entirely different—namely, one of leveling, mechanization, the development of a mass mentality and universal interchangeability of everything and everyone where no one seemed to exist any longer as himself, it was also a stimulating background. Men who could be themselves woke up in this pitiless atmosphere in which every individual was sacrificed as individual. They wanted to take themselves seriously; they searched for the hidden reality; they wanted to know what was knowable; and they thought that by understanding themselves they could arrive at the foundation of their being.

But even this thinking frequently degenerated into the frivolous veiling of reality that is characteristic of the leveling process, by perversion into a tumultuous and pathetic philosophy of feeling and life. The will to experience being for oneself could be perverted into a contentment with the merely vital; the will to find the origin into a mania for primitivism; the sense of rank into a betrayal of the genuine orders of value.

We do not propose to consider in its totality this loss of reality in an age of apparently heightened realism—an age out of whose growing awareness developed the soul's distress, and philosophizing. Instead, we shall attempt to recall by an historical account the tortuous route taken by this return to reality—a return that took many shapes —using as an example *our relation to the sciences,* an example that is inherently essential to our theme.

AT THE TURN of the century, philosophy was for the most part conceived as one science among others. It was a field of academic study, and was approached by young people as an educational possibility. Sparkling lectures offered vast surveys of its history, its doctrines, problems and systems. Vague feelings of a freedom and truth often devoid of content (because rarely effective in actual life) combined with a faith in the progress of philosophical knowledge. The thinker "advanced further" and was convinced that with each step he stood at the summit of knowledge attained up to that time.

This philosophy, however, seemed to lack self-confidence. The boundless respect of the age for the exact empirical sciences made them the great exemplar. Philosophy wanted to regain its lost reputation before the judgment seat of the sciences by means of equal exactness. To be sure, all objects of inquiry had been parcelled out to the special sciences. But philosophy wanted to legitimize itself alongside of them by making the whole into a scientific object; the whole of knowledge, for example, by means of epistemology (since the fact of science in general was after all not the object of any particular science); the whole of the universe by means of a metaphysics constructed by analogy with scientific theories, and with their aid; the totality of human ideals by means of a doctrine of universally valid values. These seemed to be objects that did not belong to any special science and yet ought to be open to investigation by scientific methods. Nevertheless, the basic tenor of all this thinking was ambiguous. For it was at once scientific-objective and moral-normative. Men could think they were establishing a harmonious union between the "needs of the mind" and the "results of the sciences." Finally, they could say that they merely wanted objectively to understand the possible world-views and values, and yet again could claim at the same time to be giving the one true world-view: the scientific.

Young people in those days were bound to experience a deep disillusionment. This was not what they had thought philosophy was all about. The passion for a life-grounding philosophy made them reject this scientific philosophy which was impressive in its methodological rigor and its demands for arduous thought, and thus at least of educational value, but was basically too innocuous, too easily satisfied, too blind to reality. Demanding reality, they rejected empty abstractions that, for all their systematic orderliness yet seemed like children's games; they rejected proofs that proved nothing despite great ostentation. There were some who took the hint implicit in the hidden self-condemnation of this philosophy which took its own measure from the empirical sciences; they pursued the empirical sciences themselves; they abandoned this philosophy, perhaps believing in another philosophy that they did not yet know.

What enthusiasm gripped those students at that time who left philosophy after a few semesters and went into the natural sciences, history and the other research sciences! Here were realities. Here the will to know could find satisfaction: what startling, alarming and yet again hope-inspiring facts of nature, of human existence, of society, and of historical events! What Liebig had written in 1840 about the study of philosophy was still true: "I too have lived through this period, so rich in words and ideas and so poor in true knowledge and genuine research, and it has cost me two precious years of my life."

But when the sciences were taken up as though they themselves already contained true philosophy, that is, when they were supposed to give what had been sought to no avail in philosophy, typical errors became possible. Men wanted a science that would tell them what goals to pursue in life—an evaluating science. They deduced from science the right ways of conduct, and pretended to know by means of science what in fact were articles of faith—albeit about things immanent in this world. Or, conversely, they despaired of science because it did not yield what is important in life and, worse, because scientific reflection seemed to paralyze life. Thus attitudes wavered between a superstitious faith in science that makes an absolute starting point out of presumed results, and an antagonism to science that rejects it as meaningless and attacks it as destructive. But these aberrations were only incidental. In fact, powers arose in the sciences themselves that defeated both aberrations, in that knowledge, as knowledge purified itself.

For, when in the sciences too much was asserted for which there was no proof, when comprehensive theories were all too confidently put forward as absolute knowledge of reality, when too much was accepted as self-evident without examination (for example, the basic idea of nature as a mechanism, or many question-begging theories such as the doctrine that the necessity of historical events can be known, and so on), bad philosophy reappeared in the sciences in even worse form. But—and this was magnificent and exalting—*criticism* still existed and was still at work in science itself: not the endless round of philosophical polemic that never leads to any agreement, but the effective, step-by-step criticism that determines the truth for everyone. This criticism destroyed illusions in order to grasp the really knowable in greater purity.

Also, there were great *scientific events* that broke through all dogmatism. At the turn of the century, with the discovery of radioactivity and the beginnings of quantum theory, began the intellectual relativising of the rigid shell of the mechanistic view of nature. There began the development which has continued to this day, of ideas of discovery that no longer led into the cul-de-sac of a nature existing and known in itself. The earlier alternative, of either assuming that we know the reality of nature in itself, or else believing that we operate with mere fictions in order to be able to describe natural phenomena in the simplest way, collapsed. Precisely by breaking through every absolute, one was in touch with every reality open to investigation.

Analogous though less magnificent phenomena occurred everywhere in the special sciences. Every *absolute pre-supposition collapsed*. For example, the nineteenth century dogma of psychiatry that diseases of the mind are diseases of the brain, was called into question. With the surrender of this confining dogma, the expansion of *factual* knowledge replaced an almost mythological construing of mental disturbances in terms of entirely unknown brain-changes. Researchers endeavored to discover *to what extent* mental illnesses are diseases of the brain, and learned to abstain from anticipatory general judgments: while they enormously extended the realistic knowledge of man, they still did not capture man.

Great, awe-inspiring investigators emerged—figures as merciless in their self-criticism as they were fertile in their discoveries.

Max Weber exposed the error in the assumption that science—e.g., economics and sociology—could discover and prove what ought to be done. The scientific method discloses facts and possibilities. To know them objectively and truly, the scientist must suspend his own value judgments in the cognitive act itself, particularly his wishes, sympathies and antipathies, although these provide fruitful stimuli and sharpen our vision on the way to cognition. Only in this way can he cancel out the obfuscation and onesidedness caused by his value judgments. Science has integrity only as *value-free science.* But, as Max Weber showed, this value-free science is in its turn always guided in its selection of problems and objects by valuations which it, science itself, is capable of recognizing. The passion for evaluation, predominant for life and indeed the basic reason why science should exist at all, and the self-conquest it takes to suspend value-judgments in the pursuit of knowledge, together comprise the power of scientific inquiry.

Such scientific experiences demonstrated the possibility of possessing a wholly determined and concrete knowledge at any given time, as well as the impossibility of finding in science what had been expected in vain from the philosophy of that time. Those who had searched in science for the basis of their own lives, for a guide to their actions, or for being itself, were bound to be disappointed.

The way *to philosophy* had to be found once again.

OUR CONTEMPORARY philosophizing is conditioned by this experience with science. The route from the disillusionment with *decayed philosophy* to the *real sciences,* and from these again to *authentic philosophy,* is such that it must have a decisive role in shaping the kind of philosophizing that is possible today. Therefore, before giving a rough sketch of the way back to philosophy, we must define the far from unambiguous relation between present-day philosophizing and science.

First, the *limits of science* become clear. They may be briefly indicated:

a) Scientific *cognition of things* is not *cognition of being*. Scientific cognition is particular, concerned with determinate objects, not with being itself. The philosophical relevance of science, therefore, is that, precisely by means of knowledge, it produces the most decisive knowledge of our lack of knowledge, namely our lack of knowledge of what being itself is.

b) Scientific cognition can provide *no goals whatever* for life. It establishes no valid values. Therefore it cannot lead. By its clarity and decisiveness it points to another source of our lives.

c) Science can give no answer to the question of its *own meaning*. The existence of science rests upon impulses for which there is no scientific proof that they are true and legitimate.

At the same time as the limits of science became clear, the positive significance and *indispensability of science for philosophy* also became clear.

First, science, having in recent centuries achieved methodological and critical purification (although this had rarely been fully realized by scientists), offered for the first time, by its *contrast* with philosophy, the possibility of recognizing and overcoming the muddy *confusion* of philosophy and science.

The road of science is indispensable for philosophy, since only a knowledge of that road prevents philosophizing from again making unsound and subjective claims to factual knowledge that really belongs to methodologically exact research.

Conversely, philosophical clarity is indispensable to the life and purity of genuine science. Without philosophy, science does not understand itself, and even scientific investigators, though for a time capable of extending specialized knowledge by building on foundations laid by the great scientists, abandon science completely as soon as they are without the counsel of philosophy.

If on the one hand philosophy and science are impossible without each other, and on the other hand the muddy confusion can no longer endure, the present task is to establish their true unity following their separation. Philosophizing can neither be identical with nor opposed to scientific thought.

Second, only the sciences, which engage in research and thereby produce compelling knowledge of objects, bring us face to face with the factual content of appearances. Only the sciences teach me to know clearly the *way things are.* If the philosopher had no current knowledge of the sciences, he would remain without clear knowledge of the world, like a blind man.

Third, philosophizing that is a pursuit of truth rather than enthusiasm must incorporate the *scientific attitude* or *approach.* The scientific attitude is characterized by a continual discrimination of its compelling knowledge— between knowledge accompanied on the one hand by knowledge of the methods that have led to it, and, on the other hand, knowledge accompanied by knowledge of the limits of its validity. The scientific attitude further requires that the scientist be prepared to entertain every criticism of his assertions. For the scientist, criticism is a vital necessity. He cannot be questioned enough in order to test his insights. The genuine scientist profits even from unjustified criticism. If he shrinks from criticism he has no genuine will to know. —Loss of the scientific attitude and approach is loss also of truthfulness in philosophizing.—

Everything works together *to bind philosophy to science.* Philosophy deals with the sciences in such a way that their own meaning is brought out and set forth. By remaining in living touch with the sciences philosophy dissolves the dogmatism (that unclear pseudo-philosophy) which tends to spring up in them again and again. Above all, however, philosophy becomes the conscious witness for the scientific endeavor against the enemies of science. To live philosophically is inseparable from the attitude of mind that will affirm science without reservations.

TOGETHER WITH this clarification of the limits and the meaning of science, there emerged the *independence of philosophy's origin*. Only as each premature assertion was exposed to the sharp light of criticism in the bright realm of science, did men become aware of that independence, and the *one primordial philosophy* begin to speak again through its great representatives. It was as if long familiar texts had returned from oblivion to the light of day, and as if men learned only now to read them truly, with new eyes. Kant, Hegel, Schelling, Nicolas of Cusa, Anselm, Plotinus, Plato, and a few others became so freshly relevant that one experienced the truth of Schelling's remark that philosophy is an "open secret." One may *know* texts, and be able to trace their thought constructions with precision—and yet not *understand* them.

From this origin we may learn something no science teaches us. For philosophy cannot arise from scientific ways of thinking and scientific knowledge alone. Philosophy demands a *different thinking*, a thinking that, in knowing, reminds me, awakens me, brings me to myself, transforms me.

But the new discovery of philosophy's origin in the old tradition immediately demonstrated the *impossibility of finding the true philosophy ready-made in the past*. The old philosophy in its past forms cannot be ours.

Although we see the historical starting point of our

philosophizing in the old philosophy, and develop our own thinking by studying it because only in dialogue with it can we gain clarity, philosophical thinking is nevertheless *always original* and must express itself historically under new conditions in every age.

Most striking among the new conditions is the development of the pure sciences we have just discussed. Philosophy can *no longer be both naive* and truthful. The naive union of philosophy and science was an incomparably forceful and in its cultural situation true cipher. But today such a union is possible only as a muddy confusion that must be radically overcome. As both science and philosophy come to understand themselves, awareness is enhanced. Philosophy, together with science, must create the philosophical thinking that stems from an origin other than science.

Present-day philosophy may, therefore, understand the sublime greatness of the pre-Socratics, but while it derives irreplaceable incentives from them, it cannot follow them. Nor can it any longer remain in the deep naïveté of the questions of its childhood. In order to preserve the depth which children for the most part likewise lose as they mature, philosophy must find paths of inquiry and verification that lie within reality as it is conceived today in all its manifestations. This reality, however, can in no instance be genuine and wholly present without science.

Although the origin speaks to us from the ancient texts, we cannot simply adopt their doctrines. Historical understanding of past doctrines must be distinguished from the appropriation of what is present in all philosophy at all times. For only this appropriation becomes in turn the ground of the possibility of an historical understanding of the distant and the strange.

PRESENT-DAY philosophizing consciously proceeds from its own source, neither discoverable nor attainable by science alone:

It carries out the quest for *reality* by means of *thinking* as *inner action*. This thinking is involved in all things, in order to transcend them to its authentic fulfillment.

This reality *cannot* be discovered once again, as in the sciences, to be a *determinate content of knowledge*. Philosophy can no longer present a doctrine of the whole of being in objective unity.

Neither can mere lived *feeling* be relied upon to make this reality present. Reality can be attained with and through feeling only in thinking.

Philosophizing presses on reflectively to the point where *thinking becomes the experience of reality itself*. To reach that point, however, I must think constantly, though without attaining reality in such thinking alone. By way of a *provisional, preparatory* thinking I experience something *more* than thought.

Philosophy is *the methodical objectification of this thinking*. I cannot provide a concept of it by giving a synopsis either of the achievements currently going by the name of the philosophy of existence, or of my own philosophy. I can only point *by way of example* to a few *basic ideas* with which it is concerned. I put the following questions:

In the first lecture: the question of *being*, in the sense of the widest *realm* of the encompassing, in which we encounter whatever being is for us.

In the second lecture: the question of *truth*, in the sense of the *way* to the being that we encounter.

In the third lecture: the question of *reality*, in the sense of being as the *goal* and *source* in which all our thought and life find rest.

✳ The Being of the
Encompassing

THE FIRST ANSWER to the question of *being* arises from the following *basic experience:*

Whatever becomes an object for me is always a *determinate* being among others, and only a *mode* of being. When I think of being as matter, energy, spirit, life, and so on—every conceivable category has been tried—in the end I always discover that I have absolutized a mode of determinate being, which appears within the totality of being, into being itself. No known being is *being itself.*

We always live, as it were, within a horizon of our knowledge. We strive to get beyond every horizon which still surrounds us and obstructs our view. But we never attain a standpoint where the limiting horizon disappears and from where we could survey the whole, now complete and without horizon, and therefore no longer pointing to anything beyond itself. Nor do we attain a series of standpoints constituting a totality in which we arrive at absolute being by moving through the horizons—as in circumnavigating the earth. For us, being remains open. On all sides it draws us into the unlimited. Over and over again it is always causing some new determinate being to confront us.

Such is the course of our progressing knowledge. By reflecting upon that course we ask about *being itself,* which always seems to *recede* from us, in the very manifestation of all the appearances we encounter. This being we call the *encompassing.* But the encompassing is not the horizon of our knowledge at any particular moment. Rather, it is the source from which all new horizons emerge, without itself ever being visible even as a horizon.

The encompassing always merely announces itself— in present objects and within the horizons—but it *never* becomes an *object.* Never appearing to us itself, it is that wherein everything else appears. It is also that due to which all things not merely are what they immediately seem to be, but remain transparent.

WITH THIS first thought we carry out *a basic philosophical operation.* With it we desire to free our sense of being from its connection with knowledge (a connection that returns in ever different form). It is a simple thought, yet seemingly impossible to perform just as it opens up the greatest prospect.

The structure of our thought forces us to make whatever we want to know into a determinate object. If we want to think about the encompassing, we must immediately make even it into something objective, such as: the encompassing is the world, is our own existence, is consciousness in general. When we think clearly about the encompassing, we thus do precisely what thinking about the encompassing is supposed to transcend. If we seek the ground of everything in the encompassing, we may no longer take any object for the encompassing; but in thinking about it we cannot avoid using determinate concepts of being. These should disappear in the execution of the thought, when we become aware of that being itself which is no longer a determinate being. Every proposition referring to the encompassing thus contains a paradox. And if it were possible to conceive something non-objective in objective form—in fact this is the basic accomplishment of philosophizing—every proposition would at the same time be unavoidably open to misunderstandings. Instead of becoming aware of the encompassing in a dynamic movement of thought, we would, in the literal meaning of isolated propositions, possess a spurious knowledge of the whole of the encompassing.

What is logically impossible to accomplish in the usual sense of knowledge is nonetheless philosophically possible as *increasing lucidity of a sense of being* totally different from all determinate knowledge. We enter the *widest realm of possibility.* Everything that has being for us in being known acquires a depth from its relation to this realm, from which it comes to meet us, announcing being without being identical to it.

THE ENCOMPASSING needs to be *elucidated further.* We must acquire the *language* which alone will allow us to formulate clearly the basic questions about truth and reality generally. The thorough development of these preliminaries to philosophizing is one of the tasks of philosophical logic. Here a very sketchy suggestion must suffice to indicate the meaning of a few words for the encompassing that are to be used in the next lecture—the words "world," "consciousness in general," "existence," "spirit," "Existenz," and "transcendence."

The one encompassing—I speak of it in this manner to elucidate its content—divides immediately into the *modes of the encompassing* through the objectivity of determinate appearances. These modes separate off as we execute the following thought-steps:

The first step:

Kant understood that the *world* does not become an

object for us, that it is only an idea; i.e., everything we can know is *in* the world, never *the* world. He saw that, if we presume to know the world as a whole existing in itself, we are trapped in irresolvable contradictions—the antinomies.

Kant further understood that all our objects are conditioned by the *thinking consciousness* (thus the unity of any given object is conditioned by the unity of consciousness-in-general as the foundation of its unity). In other words, all "being for us" is an appearance of "being in itself" as it presents itself to the consciousness-in-general that encompasses all being for us. The elaborations of the "Transcendental Deduction" aim at the one sudden shift in our sense of being: making us aware of the encompassing character of consciousness-in-general, they generate and elucidate the awareness of the phenomenality of all mundane being.

Thus the encompassing appeared in *two* modes. The encompassing in which *being itself* appears is called the *world*. The encompassing that *I am* and that *we are* is called *consciousness in general.*

The second step:

There is more to the encompassing that *I am* than consciousness-in-general. I am as *existence,* which is the basis of consciousness. The return to reality executes the step from mere consciousness to real existence—the existence that has beginning and end, that labors and struggles in its environment, or tires and gives in; that enjoys and suffers, is anxious and hopeful. Further, I am not only existence, but am actual as *spirit,* into whose ideal totalities everything thought by consciousness and real as existence can be incorporated.

The third step:

Taken together, these modes of the encompassing constitute indubitable actuality. They comprise the immanent being of both myself—existence, consciousness in general, spirit—and of my objects—the world. Whether this *immanence is self-sufficient* or points to something else is a further question. Indeed, men do leap out of immanence, in two ways at once: from the *world* to *deity* and from the *existence* of the conscious spirit to *Existenz*. *Existenz* is the self-being that relates to itself and thereby also to transcendence from which it knows that it has been given to itself and upon which it is grounded.

The articulation of the encompassing depends upon the separation of the three steps we presented one after the other: *first* the step from the general idea of the encompassing to its division into the encompassing that *we are* and the encompassing that *being itself is; second,* from the encompassing that we are to its division into what we are as existence, consciousness-in-general, and spirit; *third,* from immanence to transcendence.

This articulation thus does not mean cogent deduction from a principle, but rather an encounter at the limits. It means an acceptance of the modes of the originary presence of being.

LET US reflect upon the significance of what we have discussed so far. When the elucidation of the encompassing and its modes is successful, its effect permeates the meaning of every cognition. For it clarifies *philosophical decisions* that touch every aspect of our being.

1. The basic philosophical operation *alters my sense of being.* No longer can the totality of being be known in *ontological* concepts; in the last analysis it can be illuminated only as the encompassing realm, and as the realms in which we encounter all being. While ontology involved thinking of being as an order of objects or sense-unities, now—since Kant—every ontology must be rejected. What remains are the realms within which we

must first discover what being is. For ontology, everything was only what thought conceives it to be; for philosophizing, everything is simultaneously permeated by the encompassing, or else it is as good as lost. Ontology clarified the meaning of statements about being by referring back to a first being; philosophizing clarifies the encompassing in which everything that can be met in statements has its source and ground. Ontology attempted an objective clarification—that is, it pointed to something immediately evident in immanent thinking; philosophizing encounters being indirectly in transcending thinking. The model for the meaning of ontology is an ordered table of static categories, whereas the model for the meaning of the elucidation of the encompassing is an interlacing band of clarifying lines that move as though in suspension.

In the illumination of the modes of the encompassing a series of pseudo-ontologies inevitably arises upon which we seize. For the conceptual structure of these ontologies provides us with language. But the movement of philosophizing immediately dissolves their ontological meaning, and instead of a knowledge of a mere something causes the presence of an in each instance peculiarly colorful and open realm to emerge.

2. On the one hand, the interlacement in which being stands for us allows for an unlimited extension of cognition into everything that becomes an object. But on the other hand, in the encompassing it sets an impassable limit which at the same time gives wings to the meaning of cognition.

This has far-reaching implications, especially for our *knowledge of the reality of man*. The encompassing that I am as existence and spirit is objectified and thus becomes an object of research, as the empirical reality of human existence and spirit that comes to my attention. But scientific knowledge about existence and spirit is not knowledge of the encompassing. Rather, it is knowledge of an appearance whose being is what we ourselves are or can be, and to which we have two approaches, mutually bound to each other: through knowledge of it as appearance, and through inner awareness.

All modes of the encompassing virtually collapse when they become objects of investigation and are supposed to be no more than that. They expire in what is left when they become visible and knowable objects of research. The kind of reality possessed by a given object of scientific knowledge is a question that must be asked in any case. Negatively, it is easy to say:

No *anthropology* knows the real, living existence of man. That living encompassing existence which we ourselves are possesses biological knowledge of itself only as a perspective or uses it only as means. In our research we move about within the encompassing that we are by making our existence into an object for ourselves, acting upon it and manipulating it; but as we do this it must at the same time let us know that we never have it in hand—except for our ability to destroy this uncomprehended existence in its entirety.

No *aesthetic theory* can scientifically understand the intrinsic reality of art—that is, the truth that was experienced and created in art. What, for example, objective thinking calls "expression" and relates to a "sense of life" or character, is really a communication from the origin to a possible origin, and is encompassing reality.

No *science of religion* (history, psychology, or sociology of religion) understands the reality of religion. Science can know and understand religions without the investigator's belonging to or having faith in any of them. Real faith is not knowable.

The encompassing preserves my freedom against knowability. But if I take the content of knowledge already to be reality itself, that which is known leads me, so to speak, along a detour by-passing reality. The philosophical task within every science is positively to develop what comes to be known. All practice on the basis of knowledge must rely on the unseen encompassing: medical treatment must rely on un-understood life; planned alteration of human existence on real, un-understood faith and on the encompassing nature in the ranks of man. All true practice is therefore guided also by the encompassing, which, however, nowhere displaces knowledge. For awareness of the encompassing never cancels out the knowledge that is possible for us. Rather, this knowledge, together with its relativization, is grasped with a new profundity; for its limitless movement is incorporated within a realm, which, though it is nowhere known, becomes present as that which illuminates, as it were, all known objects.

No known being is being itself. As that which I know of myself, I am never truly myself. What I know of being is never being itself. Whatever is known has become known; it is thus a particular that we have grasped, but also something that conceals and restricts. One must continually break out of the confinement of knowledge, but one can find the content of knowledge only by unreserved and concrete mastery of cognition, which is always of particulars.

3. Whether or not I keep the *totality* of the modes of the encompassing in mind as I philosophize is a basic decision. It seems possible to grasp true being in *single* modes—in the world, consciousness in general, existence or spirit, or in a combination of these. But characteristic falsehoods and loss of reality arise in every case.

The most profoundly effective among these decisions, however, is whether I reject the *leap* from the totality of *immanence* to *transcendence*, or make the performance of this leap the starting point of philosophizing.

It is the leap from everything that can be experienced in time and can be known timelessly (and therefore always remains mere appearance) to real and eternal being itself (which therefore is not knowable in temporal existence even though it comes to expression for us only in temporal existence).

It is the leap from the encompassing that *we are* as existence, consciousness, spirit, to the encompassing that *we can be*, or authentically are, as *Existenz*. And it is thus also the leap from the encompassing that we know as world to the encompassing that being in itself is.

This leap is decisive for my freedom. For freedom exists only with and by transcendence.

No doubt there is something that seems akin to *freedom* even *at the level of immanence,* provided I do not identify the encompassing that I am as existence and spirit with its knowability. But this is only the relative freedom to remain open to the encompassing of existence and spirit.

No doubt there is also the *freedom of thought* that rises to the absolute freedom of the ability to disregard everything—the freedom of negativity. But positive freedom has another origin than has thought. It arises only for the Existenz that is reached by a leap. And this freedom is obliterated if the ability of thought to disregard is extended to freedom itself and to transcendence. I cannot disregard myself as possible *Existenz*—and therefore also disregard transcendence—without betraying myself and sinking into a void.

For the *freedom of Existenz* exists only as identity with the origin on which thought founders. This freedom is lost to me the moment I rescind the leap and slide back into immanence—for example into the deceptive idea of a universal, necessary and knowable totality of events (of the world, of existence, of spirit) in the face of which I surrender my freedom.

Here, in this leap to transcendence, I grasp in thought the basic decisions about my own being, and about its reality.

PHILOSOPHIZING in the modes of the encompassing is a matter of a *resolution*—the resolution of the will-to-being to detach itself from all determinate knowledge of being, after I have appropriated its full portent, so that being itself may truly come to me.

It is the resolution in which I determine whether I relax in a satisfying knowledge of being, or whether, instead, in an open, horizonless realm encompassing all horizons, I hear what speaks to me and perceive the flashing signals that point, warn, tempt—and perhaps reveal what is;

—whether in the reflections of being, all of which appear as representations of being, I make sure myself, and never try to avoid this route of immanence accessible to me alone, as though without it I could straightway gain access to the ground of being;

—whether I persevere until I become aware that the sole basis at the foundation of the possible *Existenz* which I am is the transcendence that supports me;

—whether, instead of gaining a deceptive toe-hold in a doctrine of being, I as an historic phenomenon become myself with the other Self within the encompassing that remains open.

THE MODES of the encompassing illuminate a basic feature of *man's* possibility.

We would like to see the *human ideal*. We would like to recognize in our thoughts what we ought to be, and what we can be on the basis of our obscure ground. It is as if in the represented image we were to find a certainty of our essence through the clarity of the idea of ideal humanity.

But every conceptual and every visible form of being human lacks universal validity. The form is only one aspect of historic *Existenz,* not *Existenz* itself. And every form of possible human perfection proves upon reflection to be defective and unachievable in reality.

Therefore, ideals serve well as guides. They are like beacons on a journey; but they do not permit us to tarry, as though our goal and rest were already contained in them.

Like everything objectively known, ideals are fused with the encompassing. Philosophizing points beyond all ideals—though only by way of and in constant touch with them—to the abiding realm of the encompassing. It is of the essence of being human to attain *consciousness of this breadth,* because the encompassing keeps us alert *to our own possibility.*

We are indeed truly human only to the extent that we always grasp what is nearest at hand, according to the standard of the ideals that have become lucid up to that moment. But thinking of the encompassing, in extending this realm, opens the soul to the perception of the origin.

For the essence of man consists not in the ideal that can be fixed, but only in his unlimited task, by the accomplishment of which he penetrates to the origin from whence he came and to which he gives himself back.

Man's essence is still less contained in the anthropological knowledge he can gain of himself as a living being in the world. Nor is it exhausted in the context of his existence, in his consciousness or his spirit. Man is all of these, and he vanishes or is stunted if one of these essentials is lost.

But although as finite temporal existence we remain veiled, and must uneasily make do from moment to moment with preliminaries, yet there is within us a hidden depth that we can feel in exalted moments, something that permeates all modes of the encompassing and that becomes certain for us precisely through them. Schelling said that we are "privy to creation"—as if in our ground we had been present at the origin of all things and then had lost this awareness in the confines of our world. In philosophizing, we are engaged in awakening the memory through which we will return to our ground. The realization of the encompassing is the first, so far still negative, step in breaking out of this confinement.

Thus far we have pointed to a *breadth* and a *depth* only in the *abstract*. Do they remain *empty,* or do we really encounter *being* in them? Consciousness of the breadth gives as such only an incentive, but not yet fulfillment. After breaking through into the realm of the encompassing, therefore, we encounter a double possibility:

Either I sink into the bottomless of the infinite: I stand in *Nothingness,* in the face of which I am what I can be *through myself alone.* If this idea does not volatilize my essence which is so problematic to itself, so that in the end I lose all sense of being, then it fanaticizes it in order to rescue me into something grasped by force, some determinate particular—blind before the encompassing and face to face with Nothingness.

Or, the awareness of the breadth engenders unlimited capacity of vision and unlimited readiness. In the encompassing, *being itself* comes out of all origins to meet me. I myself am given to myself.

Both alternatives are possible. In losing the substance of my self I sense Nothingness. In being given to myself I sense the fullness of the encompassing.

I can force neither of these two. Intentionally I can

only maintain my integrity, can prepare, and can remember.

If nothing comes to meet me, if I do not love, if what is does not come to me through my love and I do not become myself in it, then I remain in the end as an existence that can be used only like raw material. But because man is never only a means, but is always also an ultimate end, the philosopher, confronting that double possibility, and constantly threatened by Nothingness, wills fulfillment out of the origin.

 Truth

TRUTH—the word has an incomparable magic. It seems to promise what really matters to us. The violation of truth poisons everything gained by the violation.

Truth can cause pain, and can drive one to despair. But it is capable—merely in virtue of being truth, regardless of content—of giving deep satisfaction: there is truth after all.

Truth gives courage: if I have grasped it at any point, the urge grows to pursue it relentlessly.

Truth gives support: here *is* something indestructible, something linked to being.

But what this truth might be that so powerfully attracts us—not particular determinate truths but truth itself—that is the question.

THERE IS truth, we think, as if that were self-evident. We hear and speak truths about things, events, and realities that are unquestionable to us. We even are confident that truth will ultimately triumph in the world.

But here we stop short: Little can be seen of a reliable

presence of truth. For example, common opinions are for the most part expressions of the need for some support: one would much rather hold to something firm in order to spare himself further thought than face the danger and trouble of incessantly thinking further. Moreover, most of what people say is imprecise, and in its apparent clarity is primarily the expression of hidden practical interests. In public affairs, there is so little reliance on truth among men that one cannot do without an attorney in order to make a truth prevail. The claim to truth is turned into a weapon even of falsehood. Whether truth will prevail seems to depend on favorable chance events, not on truth as such. And in the end, everything succumbs to the unexpected.

All such examples of the lack of truth in psychological and sociological situations need not affect truth itself if truth is self-subsistent and separable from its realization. Yet even the existence of truth in itself can become doubtful. The experience of being unable to agree about truth —despite a relentless will to clarity and open readiness— especially where the content of this truth is so essential to us that everything seems to depend on it because it is the basis of our faith—can cause us to doubt truth in the familiar sense of something extant. It could be that the truth that matters is by its very nature not amenable to univocal and unanimous statement.

The unquestioned truth that governs my life appears false to others. In our Western world we hear conflicting claims coming from essentially different sources, and the deafening noise that echoes through the centuries as they explode into mass-occurrences.

In the face of this situation, one is inclined to accept the proposition that there is no truth. One does not allow truth to be self-sustaining; one derives it from something else as the condition on which alone truth is truth.

In consequence, thought has vacillated throughout its history: first the claim to absolute truth, then doubt about all truth, and along with both the sophistically arbitrary use of pseudo-truth.

The question of truth is one of the dizzying questions of philosophizing. As we think through this question, the magic gleam of truth is obscured.

CONFRONTED by this confusion, we quickly imagine ourselves to have a secure foundation: we conceive unequivocal truth to lie in the *validity of statements* made on the ground of visual experience and logical evidence. Despite all the sceptical subtleties, we nevertheless find the objects of the methodologically purified sciences. Through our understanding we discover cogent intelligibility and, corresponding to it, the in fact universal assent to its results on the part of every rational being who understands them. There is a realm of established correctness for consciousness-in-general, a narrow but vaguely limited realm of valid truth.

Our highly developed insight into the logical connections between the meanings of statements—a field of scientific investigation all the more intensive in proportion as it is more and more subjected to mathematical techniques (in logistics)—yet always finds that logical stringency stops when we come to the facts themselves. The truth lies in the *presuppositions* of this logical analysis; truth becomes real only on the strength of their *content*.

This content is either empirical—evident as something perceivable, measurable, and so on—in which case it is logically something that we can only accept, or it lacks this compelling power to impress itself upon everybody, having instead grown from roots which are different in essence and are the sources of those absolute contents that uphold man's life—though not every life in the same way—and that are then also communicated in statements.

Although "consciousness in general," this realm of the sciences, is also the realm where matters become clear for us because they can be stated, yet its compelling correctness is by no means ever in itself alone the absolute truth. Rather, truth emerges from *all* modes of the encompassing.

Truth that is vitally important to us begins precisely where the cogency of "consciousness in general" ends. We encounter a limit where our existence and another's existence, though both are aiming at truth as something that is one and universally valid, yet do not acknowledge that truth as one and the same. At this limit we either come into conflict, where force and cunning decide matters, or else sources of faith are communicated which approach each other without ever being capable of becoming one and identical.

At these boundaries another truth speaks. A peculiar meaning of truth emerges from every mode of the encompassing that we are, not only from consciousness-in-general, which is the locus of cogent insight, but from existence, spirit, and *Existenz* as well.

We shall present this multiplicity of truth: of existence, of spirit, of *Existenz*.

AS KNOWLEDGE and volition at the level of *existence*, truth has neither universal validity nor compelling certainty.

Existence is always particular, and wills *to preserve* and extend *itself; Truth* is what furthers existence (life), what works; falsity is what harms, limits, paralyzes it.

Existence wills *its own happiness: Truth* is the satisfaction of existence resulting from its creative interaction with its environment.

Existence, as consciousness or soul, manifests and expresses itself. *Truth* is the adequacy with which the inwardness of existence is manifested, and the adequacy of the expression and of consciousness to the unconscious.

In sum: existence grasps truth as suitable conduct, suitable first for the preservation and enhancement of existence, second for lasting satisfaction, and third for the adequacy of expression and of consciousness to the unconscious.

This is the pragmatic concept of truth. Everything that is, is in that it can be perceived and used, is raw material, is means and ends without a final end. Truth does not lie in something permanent and already known, or in something knowable, or in something unconditioned; it lies in whatever arises here and now in the immediate situation, and in what results. Just as existence itself changes in accordance with differences in its make-up and in the course of changing time, so there is only changing, relative truth.—

As spirit, truth is again not universally valid for the evidence of the understanding.

Truth of the spirit exists by virtue of membership in a self-elucidating and self-contained whole. This whole does not become objectively knowable; it can be grasped only in the action of the membership which endows it with existence and knowability.

In its understanding of being, spirit follows the ideas of wholeness which stand imaged before it, serving as impulses to move it, and as methodical system bringing coherence to its thought. *Truth* is what produces wholeness.—

Although we, being consciousness-in-general, think in terms of cogent correctness; being existence, in terms of the advantageous and threatening; and being spirit, in terms of what produces wholeness—none of this occurs in us with the certainty of a natural event. Rather, most of the time we end up in a bewildering hodgepodge. Actually, we grasp each given meaning of truth resolutely, and with an awareness of the limits of every meaning of truth, only *to the extent that we are truly ourselves.* In other words: truth that comes from any other source derives purity only from the truth of *Existenz.*

Existenz appears to itself as consciousness-in-general, existence and spirit; and it can contrast itself with their modes. But it can never take a position outside itself, cannot know itself and at the same time be identical with what it knows.

What I myself am, therefore, always remains a question, and yet is the certainty that supports and fulfills everything else. My authentic self can never become my possession; it remains my potentiality. If I knew it, I would no longer be it, since I become inwardly aware of myself in temporal existence only as a task. The truth of *Existenz* can therefore rest simply and unconditionally on itself, without wanting to know itself. In the most powerful *Existenzen* one feels this parsimony and resignation— that attains no image, no visible representation of its own nature.

THIS SHORT presentation points up the plurality of meanings of truth. We shall now *compare* these *meanings*, each of which, seen in this light, has its appropriate source in a particular mode of the encompassing.

1. Truth at the level of *existence* is a *function* of the preservation and extension of existence. It proves itself by its usefulness in practice.

Truth at the level of *consciousness-in-general* has validity as *compelling correctness.* It is by virtue of itself, and does not depend on anything else to which it would be a means. It proves itself by evidence.

Truth at the level of *spirit* is *conviction*. It *proves* itself in actuality through existence and thought, to the extent to which it submits to the wholeness of ideas, thereby confirming their truth.

Existenz experiences truth in *faith*. Where I am no longer sheltered by a certifying effectiveness of pragmatic truth, by a demonstrable certainty of the understanding, or by a protective totality of spirit, there I have come upon a truth in which I break out of all worldly immanence. Only from this experience of transcendence do I return to the world, now living both in it and beyond it, and only now for the first time myself. The truth of Existenz *proves* itself as authentic consciousness of reality.

2. Each mode of truth is characterized by him *who speaks in it* at any time. The mode of truth is given along with the encompassing within which we stand in communication.

In *existence* a purposefully and limitlessly self-interested life speaks. It subjects everything to the condition that it must enhance its own existence. It feels sympathy and antipathy in this sense only, and enters into community only on the basis of this interest.

Communication at this level is either conflict or expression of an identity of interests. It is not unlimited communication, but breaks off to suit its own purposes and uses cunning against the enemy, and against the possible enemy in the friends. It is constantly concerned with the practical effects of what is said. It wants to persuade and suggest, to strengthen or weaken.

In *consciousness-in-general* an interchangeable point of mere thought speaks. It is thought-in-general, not that of a particular individual or the selfhood of Existenz.

Its communication proceeds by rational argument. It

aims at the universal, and seeks formal validity and compelling correctness.

At the level of *spirit,* communication occurs in the atmosphere of a concrete and self-rounding totality to which both speaker and listener belong.

In the selection, emphasis, and relevance of what is said, its communication is guided by the idea—in constant connection with the meaning of the totality.

In *Existenz,* the man who is himself present speaks. He speaks to another Existenz as one irreplaceable individual to another.

Their communication takes place in a loving struggle—not for power but for openness—in which all weapons are surrendered but all modes of the encompassing appear.

3. In each mode of the encompassing that we are, *truth is opposed to untruth,* and in each a *specific dissatisfaction* finally arises, that presscs on to another, deeper truth:

In *existence,* there is the exultation of self-fulfilling life and the pain of being lost. Arising *in opposition to both,* however, is the dissatisfaction with mere existence, the boredom of repetition, and the dread in the boundary-situation of utter failure: all existence contains the seeds of its destruction. Happiness at the level of existence cannot be concretely imagined or even thought as a non-contradictory possibility. There is no happiness in duration and permanence, no happiness which, when it becomes clear to itself, continues to satisfy.

In *consciousness-in-general,* there is the compelling power of cogent correctness, the unwillingness to tolerate, and thus the repudiation of incorrectness. *Opposed to both* is the tedium of correctness, because it is endless and in itself unessential.

In *spirit,* there is the deep satisfaction in the whole and the torment of continual incompleteness. Arising *in op-*

position to both is dissatisfaction with harmony and the perplexity that results when totalities are broken.

In *Existenz* there is faith and despair. *Opposed to both* stands the desire for the peace of eternity, where despair is impossible and faith becomes the vision, that is to say, the perfect presence of perfect reality.

THUS FAR in our discussion of the various modes of the meaning of truth, the different modes simply stand side by side, and nowhere do we find truth itself.

But the modes of the meaning of truth are in no sense an unrelated aggregate. They are in *conflict:* in possible reciprocal assaults upon each other. Each truth falls into untruth when it violates the integrity of its own meaning and comes to be dependent upon and distorted by another truth.

One example must suffice: the question of the extent to which the truth of consciousness-in-general—the compelling certainty in knowledge of all that can be experienced—is useful, that is, true, for existence. If knowledge of this universally valid truth always also had beneficial consequences in existence, there would be no division, and thus no possible conflict, between the truth of existence and the truth of universally valid knowledge. But in fact, *existence constantly subverts universally valid truth* by concealing, displacing, and suppressing it. It is by no means clear whether doing this in the long run serves the interests of existence or brings about its ultimate destruction. In any case, complete acceptance and communication of the truth of universally valid knowledge is at first almost always also a threat to one's own existence. The truth of cogent correctness becomes untruth in existence. To a self-isolating will-to-existence, truth can appear as a doom to be rejected. Conversely, practical interests become a source of falsehood, in that in the medium of consciousness-in-general they deceive me into thinking that things are the way I would like them to be.

From these conflicts we acquire a feeling for the uniqueness of each individual meaning of truth—and in each conflict we apprehend a particular source of possible falsehood. If we now try to go beyond these conflicts and seek for *truth itself*, we never find it by giving *precedence to one mode* of the encompassing as authentic truth. We alternately succumb to prejudices that absolutize *one* encompassing. Thus we absolutize existence as if furthering life were the last word and could be taken as absolutely unconditioned; or we absolutize *consciousness-in-general*, the understanding, as if we could possess being itself in correct knowledge and not merely reach a perspective—a beam of light in the darkness—within the encompassing reality; or we absolutize *spirit*, as if an idea were real and self-sufficient; or we absolutize *Existenz*, as if selfhood could exist in isolation, whereas to the extent that it is itself, it comes from an other, and sees itself in relation to the other. Truth can no longer remain truth in the isolation of a single one of its meanings.

The fact that all modes of the meaning of truth *come together* in actual human life, and that man thus exists within all the sources of all the modes, urges us on to the *one* truth in which no mode of the encompassing is lost. And only clarity about the multiplicity of meanings of truth brings the question of the one truth to that point where breadth of view becomes possible, and an easy answer—in the presence of an intense urgency of the One—becomes impossible.

If the one truth were present to us, it would have to permeate all modes of the encompassing and join them all together in a present unity.

It is a *fundamental condition* of our reality that for us this unity is not attained by means of a conceivable harmony of the whole, in which every mode of the encompassing would have its sufficient as well as limited place. Instead, we remain in motion, we see every fixed harmonious form of truth once again destroyed, and we must therefore always be *seeking* further for this unity. Our knowledge would sometimes mislead us *into secluding ourselves within the consciousness* of what we at any given time systematically hold to be real and true. But in the course of time new experiences and facts befall us. Our knowing consciousness, too, must change in unforeseeable ways. For—as Hegel said—truth is in league with reality against consciousness.

The *one* truth would be accessible only in conjunction with its content—not as one kind of formal truth—and consequently in a form that binds all the modes of the encompassing together.

We cannot, therefore, directly grasp the one truth in a known whole. Grasped directly, truth is expressed formally, perhaps as the manifestness of the other that comes to meet us, then further as the being that is what it can be only through its manifestation; that is, as a manifestation that is simultaneously the realization of that being: selfhood.

But this formally expressed truth becomes *the* truth for us only along with the *content* of the realization of being. And because of the nature of our temporal existence this content becomes accessible to us as one and whole only in *historical* form. Perhaps we come closest to this form when we ruthlessly discard the traditional shells of our understanding and come face to face with the *extreme forms* of a realization of the unity of all the modes of the encompassing.

It is precisely these phenomena that, measured against

the validity and freedom of cogently valid rational knowledge, seem to us a threat to all truth: *exception,* and *authority.* The exception, by its actuality, destroys permanent and universally valid truth. And authority, by its actuality, fetters every particular truth claiming absolute autonomy.

The elucidation of the modes of the encompassing, and the experience of conflicts and incessant motion, have compellingly demonstrated that the whole truth, as universally knowable and in a single form, is neither sufficient nor actually present.

This basic situation of temporal existence *makes possible* the actuality of the *exception* as original truth in opposition to fixed universality—and it *requires authority* as the encompassing truth in historic form, in opposition to the arbitrary plurality of intention and will. Exception and authority must now be clarified.

THE MAN who is an *exception* is an exception first to *universal existence,* whether this appears in the form of the ethos, institutions and laws of the land, or the health of the body, or any other normalcy. Secondly, he is an exception to the universally valid, cogent and certain thinking of consciousness-in-general. Finally, he is an exception to spirit, in belonging to which I am as a member of a whole. To be an exception is actually to break out of every kind of universality.

The exception experiences his exceptional status, and in the end his isolation, as to him irresolubly *ambiguous* fate:

The exception *wills* the *universal* that he is not. He does not want to be an exception, but rather subordinates himself to the universal. He accepts his character as exception in his attempt to realize the universal, an attempt that now takes place not with natural *élan,* but in self-abasement, and thus fails. The exception understands himself as exception only through the universal. Because he is an exception his understanding, in his failure, grasps the positive universal all the more energetically. One who thinks from the depths of the origin, loving what he himself is not, only renders what he understands all the clearer and brighter; so clear and bright, that one who has succeeded and has become what he understands could never render it communicable.

But in spite of his subordination to the universal, being an exception in itself also becomes the *task* of finding a *unique path of realization* that makes it necessary for him to go *against* the universal, even against his will. He can lose the world in the service of transcendence, and can virtually disappear in consequence of negative resolutions (without a profession, without a family, without foundation). In so doing he can be the truth without being a model, without pointing a way for others by his own being. He is like a lighthouse alongside the road, illuminating the universal from the situation of the non-universal.

The exception can *communicate* himself: he thereby always returns to the universal. If he were certain of an absolutely incommunicable truth, it would be a truth in which no one could share. Then the exception would be as if he did not exist at all. For his communicability is a condition of his existence for us.

If, in summing up, we now ask *what* the exception is whom we find philosophically so important, he eludes us. Exceptionality is not a generic category that can be used to define a person. The word aims at a concept of a possibility that is a source of truth, running through all the modes of the encompassing and absolutely evading all definition. It is like an encompassing of everything encompassing, yet not absolute in itself, but rather approaching us in historic concreteness and at the same time repelling us even as it illuminates, sending us back to ourselves. Therefore, it cannot be objectively surveyed as a whole, nor objectively discerned, nor used as the starting point of a justification. We can perceive the exception by feeling the impact of its truth on our truthfulness; but at the same time we can fail to see it if we attempt to reckon with it as something known. Everything in the exception that becomes objectified is ambiguous both to us and to the exception itself.

Finally, if we ask *who* is an exception and who is not, the answer must be: the exception is not merely a rare borderline occurrence—as in the most extreme and soul-shattering figures such as Socrates—but is the ever-present possibility for every Existenz. By its very nature, historicity contains the exception that has become inseparably one with the universal. It is characteristic of the truth of Existenz that, throughout all forms and modes of universality, it is also always an exception.

The genuine exception, therefore, is not an arbitrary exception. This would make him a mere apostate. Rather, in his temporal existence he is inseparably bound to the truth of the encompassing. What was at first addressed in extreme situations as the most alien, and therefore as exception, is we ourselves—is every one in so far as he is an historic being, and no one in so far as every true exception is related to the universal which elucidates it. Truth is always apprehended in openness to the exception and with a view to it, but in such a way that he who apprehends does not will to be an exception. He acquiesces in being an exception, subordinating himself to the universal; he acquiesces in being the universal, knowing himself to be unimportant in the face of the sacrifice made by the exception.

AS WE penetrate to the ground of the truth we encounter within concrete actuality, we meet exception and authority. *Exception* calls everything into question, is startling and fascinating. *Authority* is the supporting, protecting and reassuring fullness.

We shall describe *authority:*

Authority is the unity of truth that binds all modes of the encompassing into one and appears to us in historic form as universal and whole. More precisely: authority is the historic union of the power of existence, compelling certainty, and idea, with the source of Existenz which in this union knows itself to be related to transcendence.

Authority is therefore that form of truth in which truth is neither exclusively universal knowledge nor exclusively external command nor exclusively idea of a whole, but all of these at once. Thus, although authority indeed comes as an external command and compulsion, at the same time it also speaks from within. Authority is a claim based on transcendence which is obeyed even by the person who at any given time commands on its basis.

The authority expressed in such formulae, however, *cannot* exist in time in a *single and universal form for everyone* without becoming superficial, without degenerating into mere power in the world of existence, becoming violent and destructive. Rather, all authority has historic form. Thus, the truth of authority can never be made sufficiently transparent, nor can its content be stabilized, scientifically, by rational generalization. Rather, it encompasses all that is knowable without destroying it.

The unconditioned character of authority thus consists in its being an *historic unity of truth* for the person living by it. On the foundation laid at the beginning, authority embraces the historic past speaking in the present, in images and symbols, in institutions, laws and systems of thought—all this by historic assimilation of the unique present that is identical with myself.

But that calm of true authority which may seem to be present in these abstract representations does not exist. Because authority is historic, and hence temporal, it is in constant *tension*, and in *motion* due to that tension.

First, there is tension between the authority that desires eternal stabilization (which, if it could reach its goal, would rob truth of all life) and the authority that *breaks out* of every fixed form to create itself anew (which, if it were to move without direction, would turn everything into chaos). Order is rooted in what has once broken out of order; the destructive exception becomes source of new authority.

Secondly, there is tension within the *individual person* between *authority* and *freedom*. At the roots of his own being, the individual wants to rediscover as his own truth what comes to him as external authority. We shall describe this process of liberation *in* authority.

At first, authority taken on faith is the *only source of genuine education affecting man's nature itself*. In his finitude each individual begins anew. For his maturing he depends upon authority in order to appropriate the content that can be handed on by tradition. As he grows up within authority, the arena in which he everywhere encounters being opens up to him. If he grows up without authority, he will indeed come to possess knowledge, he will master speaking and thinking, but he will remain at the mercy of the empty possibilities of the realm where Nothingness stares him in the face.

In the process of maturing, the individual actualizes his own origin in his own thinking and his own experience. The contents of authority come alive to the extent that he makes them his own. If this does not happen, they remain alien; rising up against them is freedom, which admits only what he can *assimilate into himself.* Freedom, which came to be by seizing on authority, can then resist authority (in determinate appearances). Having come into his own by means of authority, the individual outgrows it. A boundary concept becomes possible, of a mature and autonomous man who continually recollects, who forgets nothing, who draws his life from the deepest sources; a man capable nonetheless, with the widest vision, of acting with decisive assurance; one who, on the basis of the authority that produced him, is true to himself. During his development he needed support; he lived by reverence and obligation; where he could not yet decide on the basis of his own origin, he relied upon decisions others made for him. In the gradual process of his liberation, an inner source grew to clarity and resolute power until he heard the truth in himself with full determinateness. Now that he was liberated he seized upon this truth for himself, even in opposition to the demands of external authority. For him freedom has become the necessity of the truth that he has seized himself; arbitrariness has been overcome. Authority is the transcendence he inwardly experienced and which speaks through his selfhood.

But this frontier of the absolutely free and autonomous man can never be reached once and for all. *Every individual* fails at some time; he never becomes the whole man. Therefore, no matter how many steps he has climbed along the way to mature freedom, the honest individual cannot do without the tension between his freedom and authority; without it his way would seem uncertain and unstable to him. The contents of his own freedom clamor for confirmation by authority; or they clamor for resistance to authority; to prove themselves in that resistance becomes a sign of their possible truth, without which sign they would not be different from arbitrary and chance impulses. Authority either gives a confirming strength, or by resistance gives form and support, and prevents arbitrariness. The individual who can help himself is precisely the one who wills that authority exist in the world.

Even if many individuals were able to acquire genuine freedom in community, there would still remain the vast majority that on this road to freedom would only fall victim to chaos and to the power of its existence-impulses. Therefore authority remains necessary in the reality of the community that embraces all men, as the form of truth claiming to support all truth; or, if it is lost, authority re-constitutes itself, out of the resultant chaos, in a fateful form.

The presentation of these movements arising from the constant tension leads us back to the *encompassing authority*. Authority is the embodied riddle of the unity of truth in historic reality. The concurrence of the truth of all the modes of the encompassing with mundane power, and with the apex of human excellence that bears these truths and has this power, is the essence of true authority.

I know authority to the extent that I have grown up in it. I can live by it, but never deduce or classify it. I can penetrate it historically, but never grasp it from outside.

This authority cannot be surveyed. I do not confront it as something wholly other. But I never perceive the content of an authority that I only view from the outside and in which I have never lived—I never catch sight of it as authority.

To what authority I owe my maturing into selfhood, what authority I have seized upon and devoted myself to (though perhaps only to its remnants) is a matter of my transcendentally grounded destiny. But it is not possible to compare authorities consciously, to test them, and subsequently to choose which I think is true or best. By seeing authority as authority, I have already chosen it. Nor is it possible—on the strength of philosophical insight—to seek the true authority in the continuity stretching from the origin to the present, to will and constitute it as a goal.

Yet in philosophizing I can explain how authority *declines* and *gradually loses its power.* Authority becomes untrue when those individual modes of truth separate that belong together—whether existence, compelling certainty, or spirit—and try to become autonomous, usurping authority for themselves; when it becomes a mere power in existence without enlivening all the sources of truth; when it claims validity merely by virtue of the position of single individuals who have no power in the world, who do not make the sacrifices and do not take the risks needed to win and to maintain authority; when I relinquish the freedom of selfhood and on the strength of a supposed insight "freely surrender my freedom"; when I act in thoughtless obedience instead of yielding to the depths of authority.

IN THEIR HISTORIC actuality, *exception* and *authority* are the unfathomably encompassing. What they reveal seems nonsensical and reprehensible to the mere understanding: the one truth and the one human nature do not exist; truth, for men, exists in time and is therefore historic, therefore a task that is continually threatened.

When they occur, authoritative truth and truth uttered by the exception are the most impressive and imposing truth—and when they are lacking, men desire and long for them most desperately, with their whole being. Only where men conceal what is original and intrinsically valuable by means of a spurious clarity of the merely correct truth of the understanding does this encompassing reality of truth disappear. But it is only in this reality that I know myself as Existenz.

Exception and authority lead to the ground of truth that no longer belongs to only one mode of the encompassing but, penetrating and appearing in them all, may constitute a unity. In this unity, the conflicts arising from the struggle among the modes of the encompassing seem momentarily to be resolved—not violently by a single encompassing gaining preeminence, but through transcendence, which seems to speak as the One in all the modes of the encompassing. This is not a harmony of the modes of the encompassing, but a momentary fusion within the One that still in fact permits tension to persist and provides room for new break-throughs.

Though absolutely opposed to each other, exception and authority *belong together* as pointers to the ground of truth. Let us characterize the *common* element in their polarity once more:

1. They are grounded in *transcendence*. Where they appear, they are certain of transcendence. Without a relation to transcendence there is no existential exception and no genuine authority.

2. Both are *incomplete*. They are in motion, almost in continual self-annulment in which they in their own moment emerge from the tension as the one truth.

3. Both are *historic*, always particular and noninterchangeable. The original truth they contain thus cannot be imitated or repeated. But, since they historically enclose and encompass everything, they are in their historic concentration open in all directions.

4. Both contain truth that *eludes* formation into an observable and knowable object. If they are objectively construed, as a principle of rational deduction, exception

and authority are constricted, robbed of their life and truth. I immediately lose them if I make them into objects of my purposeful planning and action. The words "exception" and "authority" seem to denote unambiguous phenomena. But the meaning of these words refers to a transcending in which the ground of truth encompassing everything into one becomes present. Neither poetry nor philosophy master this truth. Poetry touches the border where that to which it gives form is not the ultimate inwardness with which it is really concerned. Philosophy touches the border at which its thought is never identical with the being of truth itself, though the search for truth is the ultimate purpose of philosophizing.

WHEN ONE has entrusted himself to *rationally knowable* truth in the form of concrete science—when he has further realized the meaning of truth in which he actually already lived, within the *modes of the encompassing*— and when he finally has perceived the form of truth in *exception* and *authority,* he is taking steps on the way back to reality.

But philosophically one does not reach the ultimate in either the shock given by the exception or the calm given by authority.

To live unquestioningly by authority is impossible for anyone who has ever really philosophized. It is one thing to live in authority, and quite another critically to think one's way to it. If I live in authority, truth is, in naive simplicity; if I think my way to it, however, it is infinitely complex: if one tries to give rationally adequate expression to the historic actuality of authority, no rational analysis does it justice. Yet, as one matures in philosophizing his thinking is inseparably connected with life in authority.

This philosophizing cannot deduce authority. *That* I

believe in an authority has its source in the totality of the encompassing; *whether* I should believe in it can never be proven. The elucidation of authority in general never justifies a historically determinate and concrete authority.

Philosophical thought does *not yet fall silent in the presence of exception and authority,* however. True, the paradox does not arise that authority requires justification, since every justification annuls it as authority in the act of justifying it. But philosophical thought not only undermines the deductions that become false; it may also present in the purest and clearest manner what comes from the origin.

The road that does not stop even in the presence of exception and authority, but penetrates them—the road of philosophical truth—is called *Reason.*[1] Instead of conclusively possessing truth in any of the forms discussed so far and directly exhibiting truth in its content, we shall end by speaking about reason.

To know *what reason is* by accomplishing it has always been and always will be the proper task of philosophy.

THE BASIC characteristic of *reason* is the *will to unity.* But everything turns on what this unity consists in. It is decisive for truth that the unity be seized upon as one, single, actual unity, and not as one that still has something outside it. In every premature and partial grasp of unity, one either never reaches or has already lost truth.

We have shown that truth is not one, because the exception breaks out of it, and because authority realizes

---

1. *German philosophers have long since made a radical distinction between* understanding *and* reason. *But the difference has not entered ordinary language. The profound meaning of the word reason must still be continually rewon.* (K. J.)

truth only in historical form. But as long as reason is present, the impulse to go beyond the multiplicity to the one universal truth remains undiminished, despite the spectacle of the exception, and despite obedience to authority:

The road of adequately grasping this one truth in the world of consciousness-in-general after all, as correct cognition and correct conduct according to the cogent intellectual knowledge of that world, is impassable. If I confine myself to this road, I lose the truth I live by.

Reason is often confused with the understanding because it cannot take a simple step without the understanding. But within the impulse of intellectual cognition[2]—to the *partial unities* of the level on which cogent statements are valid—there is concealed the impulse of reason to that *deeper unity* to which the unity of the understanding is only a means. The thinking of the understanding is in itself not yet by any means the thinking of reason.

Reason seeks unity, but not just any unity simply for the sake of unity. It seeks the One that contains all truth. It is as if reason brings the One from an unattainable distance and makes it present as an attracting force overcoming all divisions.

In our approach to this unity reason performs a *unifying role* in all situations. Reason seeks to bring everything back out of the dispersion of mutual indifference to dynamic interrelatedness. From the decay of mutual alienation, reason desires to bring everything back into relation with everything else. Every lack of relation is to be overcome. Nothing is to be lost.

The unifying power of reason is at work even now in the *sciences* as the drive to cross over every limit of any

2. *Verstandeserkennen.*

one science, as the seeking out of contradictions, relations, complementations, as the idea of the unity of all science.

Reason presses beyond this unity of scientific knowledge to an *all-encompassing unity*. It is reason that elucidates the modes of the encompassing, that then prevents their isolation, and presses on toward the union of all the modes of the encompassing.

Therefore, reason is concerned with what is *alien* by the standards of scientific thinking. It turns—expecting truth—toward the exception and authority. But reason does not stop even in them, as if it had reached its goal. Compared with the challenge of the One, even exception and authority are provisional; they belong to temporal existence, and are compelled by it. But reason cannot rest in anything provisional, no matter how great it may appear.

Reason is attracted even by what is *most alien*. It wants to bring into lucid being, to endow with language, and to keep from disappearing as if it were nothing, *even that which*, breaking the diurnal law, makes nocturnal passion a reality through self-destruction.[3] Reason pushes on to wherever unity is fractured, in order within this breach still to grasp its truth, and to prevent a metaphysical rupture, the disintegration of being itself, in this fragmentation. Reason, the source of order, accompanies everything that destroys order; it remains patient—incessant and infinite—in the face of everything alien, before the irruption from without or the failure from within.

Reason is, therefore, the *total will to communication*. It tends to incline toward, and to preserve, everything that can be expressed in language, everything that exists.

---

3. *Jaspers uses the terms "nocturnal passion" and "diurnal law" to refer to the voluntaristic and rational elements of life, respectively. They are roughly equivalent to Nietzsche's Dionysian and Apollonian. (Tr.)*

Reason seeks the One by way of *honesty* which, in contrast with fanaticism in the pursuit of truth, possesses an unlimited openness and availability for questioning; and by way of *justice*, which wants to let every originary thing count as itself, even while making it founder on its limits.

Reason as a content is *not a source in its own right.* It is like the source that seems to spring from the one facet of the encompassing pure and simple—to spring from it in such a way that *all the origins* of all the modes of the encompassing converge toward its openness, to be constantly related *to the One* and thus bound to each other.

In this way reason points to the source of reason: as much to the unattainable One that works through reason as to the other sources that become perceivable by means of it.

Reason is the steady advance toward the Other. It makes possible universal togetherness and involvement, and an ubiquitous listening to what speaks and to what makes reason itself speak first of all.

But reason is not indifferently tolerant of everything it meets; rather it is an open and receptive concern. It elucidates not only so as to know; it remains a questioning that is like a wooing. Reason never turns into possessive knowledge which necessarily limits and fixes itself, but remains an unlimited openness.

In its striving for the One, reason is not only able to perceive and become involved in reality, but *sets in motion* everything it touches. Because it questions and confers language, it creates unrest. Thus reason makes it *possible for all origins to unfold,* to open, to become clear, to find speech and to relate themselves. It makes it *possible for genuine conflict* and struggle to arise in and among the modes of the encompassing and to become a source of new experiences of the One.

Bound to and borne by Existenz, without which it would disappear, reason in turn makes it *possible* for the *truth of Existenz* to realize and become manifest to itself.

Although reason *does not produce anything out of itself*, it is *only because reason* is present in the innermost heart of all encompassings that it is able to *awaken all of them* and bring about their actuality and truth.

In its unlimited pursuit of the all-open will to unity that omits nothing, reason demands and risks the possibility of a *radical detachment* from everything that has become finite and determinate, and therefore fixed.

Therefore, reason quickens the negative power of the understanding to abstract from everything. Since it sees the remotest possibilities, it can even entertain the thought that it might have been possible for nothing to be at all. This thought is not just an arbitrary, empty intellectual game. In the face of the abyss, Leibnitz, Kant, and above all Schelling, could ask the question, and let themselves be moved by it: Why is there anything at all, and not nothing? Despite its rationalistic pallor, this question places us in the presence of the situation in which we first authentically experience being *qua* being as something given to us, incomprehensible, impenetrable, something that precedes all thinking and comes to meet us.

Further, the thinking of reason is only in that *movement* which knows no stopping or ending. The understanding desires security in something firmly established; it wants to know the One and to possess the Whole in a doctrine. *Reason,* by contrast, continually overthrows what has been acquired by the understanding. The unity reason strives for is not an overview of the whole, springing from a deceptive will to achieve power by means of the mere understanding. It is nothing but the drive to

surpass and bind together. There is a pride of the understanding in its possessions, but no pride of reason—only
the disclosing motion and the ultimate calm of reason.

The man who has come into his own through the
understanding is helpless when he experiences the chaos
of the overthrows and does not comprehend them through
reason. When his confidence in the understanding is
shaken, he faces the alternative: to be either less or more
than the understanding; either in the collapse of its
acquisitions, to sink down into the impulsiveness of mere
vitality, and from there to save oneself by thoughtless
obedience, or to overcome the danger by means of reason,
which melts down all truth as objective knowledge and
elevates it into the approaching truth of the encompassing.

When man reaches for his highest possibilities, he
may deceive himself most radically. He may fall down
all the steps he has climbed and end up lower than he was
at the beginning. To preserve his being he must hold fast
to every mode of reasonableness, for this alone preserves
for him the meaning of his intellectual acquisitions. In
giving up every fixation of the understanding, reason is
the condition of every other truth.

In the ideas of the all-embracing will to unity and the
surpassing and enabling *negativity,* we have expressed
fundamental features of reason. But *what reason is* has
not thereby been clarified in the same way in which a
thing can be clarified.

What reason aims at seems *impossible* to attain in our
fragmented temporal existence. Reason's goal in the One
cannot be depicted in a way that turns it into a visible
model one could follow. Instead, attracted by the One,
reason enters into the free domain of possibility, in order,
so it seems, to find its way in the abyss.

Reason—like Existenz—is reached by a *leap* out of the

closed realm of immanent things. Compared with all immanent phenomena such as the understanding, reason seems as nothing. Though reason is the encompassing that we are, in the form of a motive to seek for and realize the One, this encompassing has a transcendent source, and yet appears only in immanently experienced motives, claims, and actions.

There is, so to speak, an *atmosphere* of reason. It prevails wherever *all-open* eyes perceive reality itself, its possibilities and unlimited interpretability. Reason does not set itself up here as a judge, nor does it make any absolute doctrinal pronouncements; but with honesty and fairness it penetrates all reality and allows it to come to light. It does not explain anything away; it does not conceal or oversimplify.

The atmosphere of reason is present in the sublimest poetry, especially tragedy. The great philosophers have it, and it can still be detected wherever any philosophy at all is present. It is clearly evident in unique individuals such as Lessing, individuals who—even without substantial content—affect us as if they were reason itself, and whose words we read just in order to breathe this atmosphere.

Philosophy through the millennia is like one great hymn to reason—though it continually misunderstands itself as finished knowledge, and declines continually into reasonless understanding. As a result, it is always falling into a false contempt of the understanding, and has always been despised as an overbearing demand upon men that permits them no peace.

Reason destroys the narrowness of pseudo-truth, dissolves fanaticism, and permits no comfortable assurance based upon either feeling or the understanding. Reason is "mysticism for the understanding." Yet it develops all the possibilities of the understanding in order to make itself, reason, communicable.

Truth

IF IN PHILOSOPHIZING I desire a known content to which I can cling, if I want knowledge *instead* of faith, technical recipes for everything *instead* of an Existenz based on the whole of all the modes of the encompassing, if I want psychotherapeutic instructions *instead* of the freedom of selfhood—then philosophy leaves me in the lurch. It speaks only where knowledge and technique fail. It points, but does not give. It moves with illuminating beams of light, but produces nothing.

Just as in our description of the encompassing we ended with no more than the *broad realms* where we encounter possible being, so in the description of truth we attain nothing but *avenues* to such possibilities.

But the intent of our philosophical impulse goes much further. We do not want possibilities; we want reality.

Philosophy, of course, neither produces reality nor gives it to anyone suffering from a lack of it. But the philosopher relentlessly presses on in thought with his whole being to catch sight of reality, and to realize himself.

 Reality

As I ELUCIDATE the *realm of the encompassing* for myself, the dark walls of my prison seem to become transparent. I see the open space, and all there is can become present to me.—As I then ascertain *the truth* that is to reveal being to me, it is as if I were following the light and became free.—But as long as this light does not fall on anything, I and all things with me seem to be dissolved into unreality by its radiance. I seem to die from lucidity. I cannot love because nothing is real either in me or before me. There must be something that grows in the light of truth: the question of *reality* itself remains the ultimate question of philosophizing.

EVEN BEFORE we begin to philosophize, the *question of reality* seems to be *already answered* in every moment of our life. We deal with things, and obey the modes of reality as they have been handed down to us. There is this human existence, there are these demands and laws; human relations have an orderly arrangement and there are correct ways to govern them. Bodies exist; we find causal regularity in natural processes. Atoms exist, and energy. There are techniques for mastering nature; nature seems reliable, although the technical results of our knowledge often come about in ways scarcely different from those of primitive magic—with as little comprehension and just about as thoughtlessly.

In this unquestioning attitude we achieve a seemingly adequate view of the presence of reality. The problem arises only as I become *conscious of a lack:* when I desire reality that I neither yet know nor myself am, when this reality cannot be deliberately attained by productive and venturesome action or planning in the world, only then do I begin to philosophize. I inquire about reality.

I want to *know* true reality, as a whole, and proceed by the route of cognition.

I want *to be;* I want not only longevity, but to be my authentic self; I want eternity—and proceed by the route of efficacious action.

If we take the *first* route—the pursuit of knowledge—and desire to know what *nature* really is, we discover that whatever we conceive does not exist as such; it is a subjective appearance for us. We learned this gradually: first the perspectival foreshortening of things (in our first acquaintance with the world of astronomy); then the subjectivity of secondary qualities (color, sound, etc.), and today also the subjectivity of tangible things of space and time. Physical reality has become more and more alien. First it was conceived in terms of bodies arranged in non-perspectival space, without relation to a perceiver; then it was reduced to the underlying spatial being of particles differing from each other only quantitatively in size and motion; and finally now nature cannot even be imagined, but can be described only in mathematical formulae. As we came to know an unfathomably remote reality accessible only to measurement, the world began at the same time in a mysterious way to take on the character of "appearance" for us. In the end we were able to take this appearance for full reality once more, but in such a way that now "true" reality is nowhere. Everything is real in its own way, and at the same time everything is only a perspective.

The same thing happens to our knowledge of *human existence*.

Men believe that they understand their own existence realistically, whether in terms of economic facts, or of diplomatic and political action, diverse social systems, spiritual principles, etc. By declaring certain connections to be basic and deriving the rest from them as secondary superstructures, men are caught in a consciousness of reality that quickly decomposes in the light of critical knowledge. All these objects of investigation are indubitable factors; but again "true" reality cannot be encountered with them anywhere. Neither investigatable objects nor the sum-total or any arrangement of them ever comprises the whole.

Although reality seems *to recede continually* as we gain determinate knowledge, so that the question of what reality is can in principle never be answered by critical investigation, yet *individual facts* seem to remain as real. A fact—so it is said—either exists or does not exist; here is something unshakeable; here mutually opposing and even hostile views must recognize something common to them all; what exists, what has happened, what is done, must always be known, or at least knowable, to someone. But this is an error. In the *first* place, every actual individual thing is *inexhaustible*, and *secondly* every fact is subject to *unlimited interpretation and re-interpretation*. If one desires to grasp a fact in a determinate way, he will have to construct it. "All facts are already theories." Every single fact remains inexhaustible and subject to further interpretation, even when one has removed all deception, patent falsehood, obfuscation, suppression and secrecy.

Whether I try to apprehend reality as a whole or as a single fact, in the end it is always the *unattainable limit* of methodical research.

On the *second* route—of action—we seek reality as our own being.

Our *existence* as such leaves us unsatified in its continual and endless drive for more, a drive that lacks a final goal and increasingly realizes its own meaninglessness as it clearly forsees its own end. In deed, work, fame, and our effects on posterity we gain only a second duration for a slightly longer term; but we cannot conceal from ourselves the fact that this second temporal duration, too, has its absolute end in the silence of the universe.

Next we look for the reality of our own being in our *selves* as independent beings. But the more resolutely we are ourselves, the more decisively we learn that we are not ourselves through ourselves alone, but that we are given to ourselves. Even our own authentic reality as Existenz is not "ultimate" reality.

AS WE TRY to attain a conscious apprehension of reality by these routes, so that in the end we either would *know* it or *be identical with it ourselves*, we fall into an abyss. In this way we neither know reality as something other than ourselves nor do we possess it in ourselves. All routes—to the concrete sciences, to things themselves, to a subsisting object, to any kind of ontological knowledge—lead us, if we confine ourselves to them, only *to modes* of reality through modes of knowledge that prove to be inadequate.

Up to this point our philosophizing has only been clearing away difficulties. On the basis of this *critical* philosophizing we are looking for *another* kind of philosophizing in which we find the way back to reality. We are seeking a philosophizing that starts by granting all the possible modes of reality, i.e., that desires to grasp and know them without limit, but transcends them to *reality itself*. And there is the rub! Here philosophizing must prove itself. How this is accomplished can be shown only in the concrete process of philosophizing itself. For lack of space, examples must suffice. I shall choose abstract, speculative thinking in the narrow sense, and shall try to make its meaning evident merely by intimation:

AUTHENTIC reality is the being that *cannot be thought in terms of possibility*. What does this mean?

Any actuality, whose existence I comprehend through the causes that produced it, could have been different under different circumstances. Considered simply as something known, any known actuality is a *realized possibility;* as an object of thought it retains the character of possibility. Even the whole world, considered as an object of my thought, is one of many possible worlds. To the extent that I know reality, I have posited it in the realm of possibility.

When we are dealing with reality itself, however, possibility ceases. Reality is that which can no longer be translated into possibility. Where what I know is one of many possibilities, I am dealing with an appearance, not with reality itself. I can think about an object only if I think of it as a possibility.

Reality is therefore what resists all thought. Schelling expressed this idea: "The truly existent is precisely that which strikes down whatever comes from thought." (Schelling, II, 3, 161.) Thought by itself cannot reach reality. It runs aground on reality. Only through the recoil of its inability can it make us feel that the crux of the matter is a leap into reality.

A completely thinkable reality would not be reality any longer, but only an *addendum* to what is possible. It would not be an origin, and therefore the real thing, but something derivative and *secondary*. And indeed, we are overcome by a feeling of nothingness the moment we imagine that we have transformed all of reality into conceivability; that is to say that we have put this total conceivability in the place of reality. Then the thought that there need be no reality is a sign that the nothingness of conceivability is sufficient to itself. But it is not sufficient to us, who in this nihilation of reality experience our own nihilation. Rather, the awareness of reality liberates us from the illusory world of what is merely thinkable. As we make contact with reality in transcending, thought is to us not primary; rather, since thought must be understood in the actuality of the thinker and in its recoil in the presence of the unthinkable, it is derivative in comparison with reality. "It is not because there is thought that there is being," says Schelling (II, 3, 161n.), "but it is because there is being that there is thought." If thought doubts even reality, Schelling answers in the presence of this unthinkable, preconceptual, primordial reality: "The infinitely existent, just because it is this, is safe against thought and all doubt" (II, 3, 161).

In addition, the *thinker's reality* is prior to his thought. We are *masters of our thoughts*. To the extent that we are real we do not subordinate ourselves to a system of thought or to an idea of being. What I think is possibility, also in virtue of the fact that I can either embrace it or let it alone. No matter what I think, my own being as a whole is not contained in any thinking or thought. Rather, my thinking is subordinate to my reality, unless this reality is not I myself but an aspect of my empirical ex-

istence, which in turn has rightly to subordinate itself—
or else, unless I am not myself at all but have given up my
reality and am indeed unwittingly subject to something
else, whatever it may be.

Since reality *as thought recedes* from us while nonetheless being present as the all inclusive *bearer,* and since
its presence consists in what no thought can turn into a
possibility, *philosophical thought* means not that we void
the *inconceivability* of authentic reality, but that we *intensify* it. The force of the real is made palpable by the
foundering of thought.

Speculative thought must be defended against *misunderstanding:*

With the thought of the real that does not become possibility, I think my way to reality. If one uses the category of possibility to transcend to reality, both possibility
and reality cease to be categories. If, however, we again
turn them into determinate categories, that is, use them
as concepts to acquire a knowledge of reality beyond all
possibility, instead of using them to transcend to the unthinkable, we then have a pseudo-knowledge of the
known necessity of the real. This deterioration of the
transcending meaning into a possession of knowledge
shows itself in the way we inwardly experience these
thoughts (for mere thoughts apart from any relation to
experience are empty anyway):

We are uneasy in the presence of an allegedly *known*
reality without possibility. For our movement through
possibility is the very breath of our temporal existence, is
a condition of our freedom. Brutal facticity, inescapable
necessity, unambiguous things in being, if they are held
to be absolute reality in the form that we know them,
overpower and suffocate us.

In genuine transcending, however, where we do not
allow the thought to slip back into finite knowledge, it is

precisely the possibilities in every appearance, in everything we can conceive, and in the ambiguity of appearing facts, that remain inviolate. Only as we move through these possibilities in our temporal existence do we come to a peace that is no longer a paralyzing malaise in the presence of facticity without possibility, but is the wonder before eternal being as it reveals itself in the infinity of temporal appearances, and is the profound satisfaction in this wonder.

As soon as I think, I am again in the realm of possibility. Therefore, on the one hand, thought always provides us with the domain of possibility in temporal appearance where our freedom and our hope have their stay; and therefore, on the other hand, thought stops in the presence of eternal reality without possibility, where we do not need freedom any longer, but find peace.

WE SHALL attempt to make reality perceptible by a second example: *Reality appears to us as historicity*.

Eternal reality can be encountered neither as a *timelessly subsisting other*, nor as something *permanent in time*. Instead, reality is present *to us* as a *transition*. It acquires existence in the imminence of departing from existence. It attains neither the form of lasting duration nor that of unchanging order, but only that of foundering.

This nonsubsistence and transitional character of phenomenal reality can be described:

1. *Man* is the nothingness of a speck of dust in the limitless universe—and he is a creature of a depth capable of cognizing the universe, and of encompassing it within himself. He is both, between both. His faltering being is *not an extant, determinable actuality*.

2. *Human history* has no possible end-state, no lasting completeness, no goal. At any time a *completion* is possi-

ble that is at once *end* and *decline*. The greatness and essence of man stand under the condition of their moment. *Reality reveals itself only to the transition*—and does so not in the arbitrary moment of a mere occurrence, but in that fulfilled moment which is an unrepeatable, noninterchangeable presence of reality itself even in its evanescence, and which has been decided for the Existenz standing in it, and in its afterglow also for the spectator who reaches for this inconceivable reality with his understanding.

3. The *reality* of the *world* does not become a whole with which man could become identical and thereby achieve authentic being. When construed as the world, reality is always already lost. *Ideas of perfection* regarding the whole display only a deceptive *harmony,* whether in the form of a definitive ordering of a transparent reason, or of the whole of a universal life, of the continual emergence of justice from conflict, or a cyclical series, of the history of a fall and subsequent necessary restoration, or however conceived.

Situated between nothing and everything, continually merely in transition, lacking the perfectability of an all-encompassing totality, in every instance man is *real* only as *historic*. Conceiving reality as historicity does not mean knowing its history and then regulating one's actions on the basis of this knowledge (for example, by deducing both the task of the present age and my own task within it from knowledge of the place of this age in a whole of history). Rather, it means *penetrating to the origin* by *becoming one* with the *temporally concrete appearance of the reality* in which I stand.

There are *many ways to formulate this*. All are misunderstood if they are taken as rules of conduct; but they remain true if taken as indicating the modes of historic awareness of reality: to fulfill the moment; to meet the challenge of the day; to carry out one's unique function; to be wholly present. Further: to discover the depths of the present in its foundations in the past, and in the realm of possibilities from which the future is coming: recollection and vision of the future become the reality of the present, and not remote concerns that we use to escape from the present. They raise the present into an eternal present. Reality is only in the present, and as such, historic, unrepeatable.

Only through historicity do I become aware of the authentic being of transcendence—and only through transcendence does our ephemeral existence acquire historic substance.

LET US TRY A THIRD example: authentic reality is for us only if it is *one*.

Every *unity* is at first *lost* when the world is clarified by our knowledge of actualities:

1. All progress in knowledge shows ever more decisively that the *world* as we know it contains *discontinuities between the modes of being*. As our knowledge becomes clearer we find a gaping chasm between inorganic nature and life, between nature and life, between life and consciousness, between consciousness and spirit—and yet above and beyond all these discontinuities there is a union and a unity that, although constantly receding, is the presupposition and task of knowledge.

2. Man is not able *correctly to order* the world as a whole into a *unity*, in the sense of giving a final and permanent duration to his existence. Every one of his world-arrangements soon proves to be impossible, to contain the seeds of its own destruction, and to strive restlessly on into the immeasurable—and yet we strive incessantly for the one, unifying and self-sustaining arrangement.

3. Where man becomes aware of his own *selfhood* as an origin, he also becomes aware at once of *fragmentation*, first in his inability to realize this selfhood completely and give unity to his existence, and secondly in the plurality of truths of the *Existenzen* that encounter one another. And yet the essential feature of Existenz itself is its desire to push on in communication to the One that binds even the most distant people together and to which everyone belongs.

Every mode of fragmentation of being is a *demand* upon us *not to see reality itself in the fragments*. The drive of our reason to unity counts as genuine reality only what is encountered in unity, not in dispersion or in these preliminary pluralities. One God, one world, one totality of natural phenomena, one truth, the unity of the sciences, historic oneness in the world wherever something is essential to us—these are demands that must be fulfilled, or else not only does chaos result, but the isolated parts seem to lose their reality.

But in trying to understand unity we continually fall *into error*. We are inclined to take some *restricted truth for the one truth* (and thereby absolutize the compelling validity of correct intellectual knowledge of finite things in the world into truth in general); or we take the *world as a whole* to be cognoscible in a uniform way (and absolutize a relative whole of physical or biological cognition into the whole of being itself); or we unnoticeably cling to the pre-supposition that only *one mode of humanity* is the true human ideal (and thereby absolutize an historic form).

As a matter of fact, unity cannot be directly understood as something immediately given, as an item of knowledge, an idea, or an institution. Every road toward becoming aware of being itself as a merely immanent being leads to breaches, discontinuities, discrepancies, incompleteness. Even our most resolute self-awareness arises along with the fundamental knowledge that as possible Existenz we can become ourselves only with another Existenz: even Existenz is not a self-contained unity. If there is *unity*, it is *only in transcendence*. From the standpoint of transcendence, unity can be apprehended in the world; we can feel the one God in the unconditioned, exclusive unity of our self-realization. In transcending all immanent unity, unity is reality itself. True unity, as the pivotal point on which all changing unity in the world turns, and as the archetypal unity of all visible and reflected unity, is in transcendence.

IN EACH OF our three examples we were led to *similar experiences:*

1. Reality *recedes*, until it *stands firm* only in transcendence.

Each time we apprehended reality in *determinate* knowledge, the question arose all over again: what is *reality itself* and how is it present? I lose transcendence when I *anticipate* it and think I already have it in some intelligible world. When we philosophize we must resist the inclination to identify reality with what is palpably present, to possess it in forms that we contemplate, to desire to know it rationally and reliably in speculative thought. It is always the same: when one wants to grasp reality directly, when he speaks about it immediately, and imagines that he knows it in thought—instead of touching it in transcending as he realizes his own Existenz—just when he believes himself to be on the verge of grasping it by critical and skillful operations, it is in the habit of withdrawing.

2. The route philosophizing travels toward reality illustrated in the examples was a *kind of thinking that uses categories to go beyond categories*. Categories—such as

unity, possibility, etc.—are the determinate forms of objects for us. In transcending these categories we seem to conjure up reality. In our thinking, we would like to press on to the point where thought is identical with reality; but as we do so we experience the blow of thought rebounding from reality. As thinking transcends itself in the experience of this blow, it can make reality present to the thinker in an indirect and irreplaceable way.

3. It is a fundamental experience that reality does not simply "exist." As long as we measure by the standards of what is conceivable to us, of completeness, correctness and duration, there is always something *wrong* with the way reality appears to us. It is as if we had fallen from reality, and returned to it only by means of truth.

Therefore, every temporal appearance of reality is also inadequate. Whatever exists, it must become something else.

And therefore what we know directly of immanent being is an appearance of reality only if it is *transparent*.

If now—misunderstanding our three examples—we understand speculative thought as though, instead of helping us to transcend, it allowed us to know *reality* itself by means of *finitizing conceptions,* we *pervert* thought into an opaque and immanent set of rational contents:

Brute fact is not reality without possibility. If we remove possibility from any immanent being and then absolutely posit it as a knowable reality, we cause transcendence to disappear, freedom to weaken, and we deceive ourselves about reality.

The *historical and visible objectivity of particular individuals* is not the historicity of Existenz. To identify historicity, in the form of the historical plurality and particularity of existence, with absolute reality is to cause transcendence to disappear into mere willfulness.

No conceivable form of *unity*—whether numerical or

logical—is the unity of absolute reality. An objective unity in the world, known, objectified, and insisted upon as such, is no longer the transcendent unity, but something that is restricted, isolated, mechanical or systematic.

And yet transcendence is present only where possibility ceases; it is not present in time without historicity; and it does not lack unity.

4. Reality and the experience of reality are not at all self-evident. Of course, at any moment it seems possible for reality to be present, but for the most part reality seems to have vanished. Opinions, notions, customs, and vital feelings are the unreliable bearers of a phantom reality.

Confronting reality, therefore, is always like *breaking out of illusion.* It is a new, authentic and supporting experience.

I attain this experience of the real only if I *become myself.* Transcendence is inaudible as an experienceable mundane being; its voice is audible only to Existenz. My own reality is determined by the *way* I know and *what* I know reality to be. Our proximity to reality is constituted by the ways we encounter reality beyond possibility, and apprehend its unity in and through our historicity.

Corresponding to the depth, power, and extent of our realization of Existenz there are, as it were, degrees of presence and therefore of reality, of proximity to and remoteness from transcendence.

5. In every *inadequacy*—that is, wherever reality is not present in its depths—we are prompted to feel that man attains *peace* only in the being that is reality itself.

A source of wonder and satisfaction lies already in the mere fact *that anything exists.*

But the crucial point is: *what* exists. We are not aware of reality in the empty peace of unconcern with facticity, but only in the peace that overcomes the concern caused by the facticity of reality—that is, in an acquired, fulfilled peace.

Though peace can be found only in reality, this reality is audible to me in time only in the language of finitude. The form in which I think about reality in times of extreme need, at the boundary, is a basic feature of my own reality. Ultimate satisfaction can be attained only in *reality itself*, infinite and perfect, out of and in which both we and every thing for us exist. But we are aware of this reality always *only by means of appearances* in concrete historic situations.

ALL THE EXPERIENCES we have discussed converge: in existential thought I make *fundamental philosophical decisions* according to *how I apprehend reality*:

1. The first decision of philosophical faith is whether it is possible to think of the *world as complete in itself,* or whether *transcendence* guides our thought.

The claim of pure immanence is grounded on the assertion that everything transcendent is a delusion, an illusion of impractical people, an imaginary something used to escape from the harshness of reality.

Immanence imposes itself as being itself, because it alone is knowable. Only immanence can become known —and all knowledge concerns only immanence.

Yet because of its divisions, its fragmentation, its lack of unity, the plurality of its appearance, and its incompleteness, immanence proves to be fragile.

In spite of all the momentary power and the momentary clarity of its knowledge, mere immanence is opaque and superficial, lacking the unconditional quality of loyalty, the continuity of growth in loving struggle, and the presence of authentic reality. It remains in a hopeless and self-concealing struggle for existence, ending in nothingness. Even love, if it remains merely immanent, lacks the powerful wings that would permit it to soar and love all things worthy of love more clearly and profoundly, as if only now all being were revealed—it becomes a restricting passion.

Whatever does not reach transcendence seems forlorn; it merely runs its course and is either unconscious of itself or conscious of itself as nothingness. The moment I allow being to be absorbed without remainder in what is known, transcendence has vanished from me and I am opaque to myself.

Accordingly, there is a radical shift in our consciousness of being the moment we come to experience originally, with our whole being, that transcendence is for us the *reality that shatters all existence.*

Although concealed, transcendence is present in philosophizing as reality. But what transcendence seems to say is always ambiguous. I must take my chance on the basis of a responsibility that is not annulled by any direct revelation from God. Transcendence is the power through which I am myself: where I am truly free, it is precisely because of transcendence. Its most decisive *language* is the one which speaks through my freedom.

2. The second decision is whether transcendence leads me out of the world to a *denial of the world,* or whether it requires me to live and work only *in the world.* Philosophical faith is bound to the world as the condition of all being for it (so much so that in fact philosophy is in constant danger of being made vacuous by a doctrine of pure immanence). It demands that one stay with things in the world and allow nothing to take precedence over doing with all his powers what is required here (in order to perceive the ever-ambiguous language of transcendence in the world and in the reality arising within it), and at the same time never to forget the evanescence and noth-

ingness of the whole in the presence of transcendence. In addition to the knowledge of finitude, philosophical faith demands historicity as the sole mode of realization. It demands a highminded attitude that does not "will" death, but assimilates it in its power to force us wholly into the present. If philosophy means learning how to die, it does so not in the sense that I lose the present in the anxiety produced by the thought of death, but rather in the sense that I intensify the present by undiminishing and active fulfillment under the standard of transcendence.

Hence, transcendence means nothing to us if all there is for us takes the form of existence.

Hence, also, transcendence means everything to us if every existing thing that has true being for us has it only in relation to transcendence or as a cipher for transcendence.

IN THIS KIND of philosophizing our ascertainment of reality is expressed, but not yet achieved, in thought. Philosophy seems to be an ineffectual and disappointing kind of thought; nowhere does it give "true" reality. For it pre-supposes that by philosophizing the thinker only wants to heighten the clarity and reliable continuity of *what he brings with* him and *can be,* and not that he wants to obtain something that he never knew and by himself could not be. The last step on the return to reality must be taken *by each person himself* in ways that cannot be anticipated. All we can do philosophically is point the *way* by which one can approach reality through truth and apprehend being, which is always present and yet is never generally manifest.

Religion gives rise to entirely different hopes. The reality that supports everything is experienced in religion as certain, guaranteed by authority, and the subject of a completely different kind of faith from that of philosophizing. Reality has spoken, and is apprehended in *myth* and *revelation*.

Philosophy cannot produce *myth*. For where myth occurs reality itself is present in it. Philosophy can only play in myths and indirectly come to certainty. It cannot take the place of *revelation*. For if there is revelation, reality itself speaks in it; philosophy can only keep silent if reality is present here—but it will immediately reflect on the accompanying propositions, claims, sensible phenomena, and demands in the world.

We shall *characterize religion* as it appears when seen from the point of view of philosophy, hence from outside. Although these aspects of religion inevitably arise, one must admit that they are not adequate characteristics of actual religious faith and may even miss it completely. We shall select a few features from these characteristics. The three examples previously discussed, of philosophical transcending to reality, will serve as guides.

1. Wherever *reality without possibility* is present, it must acquire a *language* and become capable of being addressed, if it is to be there for us. But since language is thought and its contents are ideas, language would at once think about reality in a way that again turns it into a possibility actualized from among other possibilities.

If language is to express the indubitable facticity of reality it must take on the *form* of thought that at the same time ceases to be thought.

Myths and fairy tales are instances of such a form. A story is told, not with a pragmatic intention (i.e., of making events comprehensible by constructing an adequate network of causes and motives, and thus making them into something that could just as well have been different), but as an indubitable event the telling of which makes reality alone palpable as a "thus it is" or "it happened thus," without the question about another possibility arising in the astonishment. Reality is simply received as incomprehensibly self-evident. Something visual, without concepts or the generality of thought, is here the form in which the whole of reality is felt. It is precisely when they explain nothing and are meaningless by the criteria of rational consequence, causality and end, that myth and fairy tale can have great depth and infinite interpretability.

Myth and fairy tale are only one form of the language of reality. In general one may say: Reality is that which can *be narrated only in the form of a story;* e.g., that anything exists at all rather than nothing, the facticity of the actual world, the primordial phenomena as an appearance of this reality.

Only the *language of imagination*—so it seems— touches reality that evades all objective investigation.

Only by *attending to the ciphers of being* can one perceive this indubitable reality; it is as if in the act of attending a transformation occurs: not only into transparency, but into the ungrounded necessity that is no longer the opposite of possibility.

The language of transcendent reality is an objectivity having an incomparable and underivable origin:

For philosophy, it is the language of *ciphers.* For religion, it is the actual presence of transcendence in *myth* and *revelation.*

The usual alternative, which admits only either an *unreal symbol* of imagination or a *sensible-corporeal actuality,* prevents us from appreciating this basic fact and its origin.

Actually both occur:

On the one hand a sensible *reification,* as for instance in the risen Christ, who passes through locked doors, suddenly appears to his disciples and has Thomas, who up to that time was skeptical, poke a finger into his wounds—and on the other hand the *volatilization* into aesthetic symbols which preserve a non-committal fascination without any real presence, but offer themselves for our enjoyment in ever-different forms out of the infinite abundance of historical tradition.

But in opposition to both alternatives—or rather antecedent to both—is the element of originality: Reality cannot be apprehended in any other way than by *believing perception*, believing experience. It is present, but only when one can perceive it from the depths of his own selfhood.

Psychologically, it is a matter of images by which faith encounters reality. I fall into error if I hold fast to these images and think I can acquire faith ready-made in their presentation: the reality present in faith eludes me. For faith is not a matter of images, but of the reality of what is believed. Just as the world's actuality is accessible through the senses, that of transcendence is accessible through faith—either philosophical or religious—in each case as "the other." An errant idealism transforms both the world of the senses and that of faith into an illusion, and makes them into creatures of consciousness. But philosophy stands in the presence of reality.

The genuine presence of transcendent reality is therefore not destroyed by an "enlightenment." The clearest investigation of the sense-world can only enhance the genuine perceptibility of transcendence as it demolishes superstitious fixations and confusions.

It is a characteristic tendency of *religion*—so far as one can see from a philosophizing standpoint—to encounter transcendence as a sensible and particular object in the world, that is, as the specifically sacred object. For philosophy, on the other hand, the perception of transcendence can occur in every form of sensibility and empirical actuality, for the location and ground of this perceptual capacity is freedom in its historically multiple forms. In principle everything can become sacred, and nothing is exclusively sacred—generally and for everyone. In other words, in religion the symbolical reality of the cipher seems to be made into a finite sensible reality of the supersensible—as in aesthetic contemplation it is reduced to the emptiness of mere signification. The rejected alternative involuntarily arises again if the cultic, dogmatic, and institutional forms of the contents of religion are viewed from the standpoint of philosophy. The philosophical thinker may be able to be bound to the symbols of his religion, perhaps even with an extraordinary inwardness. He wards off every violation of them. The symbols can speak to him in irreplaceable ways, and can become signs to him of reality that is all the more unfathomable the more he desires to interpret it. But these symbols cannot preserve for him the exclusiveness of the specifically sacred. They remain truly symbols for him only if they are infinite, that is, if they cannot be enclosed in any dogmatism or purposeful action.

For philosophy the ciphers are the form of transcendent reality in the world. Everything in the world can be a cipher and nothing is of necessity a cipher for the understanding. The cipher cannot be interpreted by means of anything else. But it ceases to be a cipher and becomes an empirical reality if it demands to be perceived as a separate and tangible form of sacredness that isolates itself in the world.

2. Philosophically, transcendence can always be understood *historically*, and comes to be present only historically. This means, however, that its *objective* appearance cannot become valid and true *for all men*. For the revealed faith of religion, on the other hand, transcendence

is contained in a historical, unique form that is objective for all, exclusively valid, and the condition of salvation for everyone.

From the standpoint of philosophy this is a *transformation of historicity itself*. Since the profundity of belief in revelation consisted in its apprehension of the impassable ground of existential faith in its historicity, this transformation may lead to the loss of existential historicity itself. For existential historicity must deny to itself its immediate transcendent source if instead of living in my factual historicity, I let it become submerged in one single universal historicity. If I believe in the absolute reality of one historicity—which in itself is also merely particular—and which is supposed to absorb all historicity, I break off possible communication with other historicity, so as to force the other into my own, as material.

What is granted to everyone as his historicity, his recollection, his One, what stands before him at the boundary, is indeed inseparably linked with a common tradition. This tradition becomes more profound, alive and concentrated the more it incorporates into its own recollection a historicity broadened to include the plurality and incessant dynamism of all human possibilities and actualities. But this common tradition— viewed philosophically—must not be absolutized into the single absolute world historicity for all: first, because other historicities have their own rights by virtue of their own origins, and their spirit should not be destroyed but have a voice in the temporally unending process of questioning and being questioned; secondly, because the irreplaceable historicity of the individual should not cause the immediacy and autonomy of its transcendent origin to be obliterated by being subsumed under the generality of a single world-historicity.

It is the transformation of that Existenz which is not enclosed within itself, but realizes itself historically in freedom and openness to every origin and to the immeasurable, into the Existenz that confines itself within a determinate fulfillment that denies all other origins and is made obligatory for all men and all times. To philosophy it here seems that reason has been abandoned.

3. Even the One appears transformed in religion— viewed from the standpoint of philosophy. It has become a visible, objective unity in the world. In the belief in revelation, I apprehend the One as that unity which is the One for all men in this particular historic form and which in spite of its historic character universalizes its historic objectivity. I believe in this unity in the traditional institution of the church as an encompassing sensible and visible object. No longer do I belong historically to *my* church, but absolutely to *the* church, which alone is universal and true. Then the present is no longer an appearance of one historic Existenz among others, but is the all-inclusive whole. The following results indicate the character of this unity:

Authority is no longer engaged in historic struggle but, because it is one, it is also absolute, and fixed: —

I believe in one book out of the past, not in the way I give credence to the great contents of other books, but as the one, single book through which God directly revealed himself; and I believe this because the present church as its visible warrant pronounces it to be the single, sacred book and demands this faith; —

I must hold all other kinds of historical faith to be false, true only to the extent that scattered seeds and fragments of truth live in them, but which have become really clear and true only in the one church; —

There is no salvation for me or for other men outside the one true church; —

Unity no longer exists in a fragile way, but materially and perfectly; it is to be found in this form of the single, visible and holy church and in the absolute satisfaction gained by participating in it.

ALONG WITH this characterization of religion in terms of its difference from philosophy—even if this characterization were not limited to a few features but were completely developed—and in the presence of the monumental historical actuality of religion, *questions* arise which cast doubt upon the meaning and power of philosophizing because of its distance from reality.

The first question:

Religion is attested to by heroism in suffering and action, through artistic creations and poetry, by an extraordinary kind of thinking deposited as theology. Through its creations the reality of this faith in transcendence brings the reality of transcendence incomparably near.

Can I in philosophizing hold as resolutely to reality as I can in religion? Does philosophy in itself have that reality which I can live by, and which, like religious reality, stands firm in every situation?

The *answer* is: Religious reality is not attainable through philosophy. It is other, perhaps more, than philosophy can represent or grasp. Philosophy has nothing comparable to the positive quality of religion. Nevertheless, philosophizing is *not without its positive quality*, though one whose basic character seems to a philosopher threatened, if not lost, in religion.

Philosophical faith is the substance of a personal life; it is the reality of man philosophizing in his own historic ground, in which he receives himself as a gift.·

In philosophizing I experience the reality of transcendence unmediated, as that which I myself am not.

Though incapable of being contained in any institution

while perhaps possible in all, philosophical faith speaks and lives in the communication of the philosophical spirit realm—in this transforming, understanding conversation between thinkers—in this appearance of the one perennial philosophy which is never finally grasped and which in spite of hostility and basic differences binds men together into a whole in which all participate but which is no man's property.

Philosophical faith is the indispensable source of all genuine philosophizing. From it comes the striving of individuals in the world to experience and investigate the appearances of reality with the aim of attaining the reality of transcendence ever more clearly. But source, striving and aim are realized only for a time in historic, unrepeatable form.

Because it is undogmatic, philosophical faith—in which reality is grasped—is amenable to no confession of faith. For this faith, thought is the passage out of the dark origin into reality. As mere thought it is therefore without value, meaningful only through its efficacy in illuminating and presenting possibilities, through its character as inner action and its conjuring power.

The second question:

Our attempt to characterize religious reality has been made from the viewpoint of philosophy, not from a participation in religious reality itself. Does it not display from the start an attitude of *rejection* of religion and a *suspicion* that there is something fundamentally wrong about religion, something that is fundamentally not true? Is it not already an *attack upon religion*?

To this question we can *reply* that whenever one speaks about religion from the viewpoint of philosophy, or about philosophy from the viewpoint of religion, it must seem to the object that the characterization is inadequate. Philosophy and religion are understood only by those who are themselves by virtue of their respective faith, either philosophical or religious. It would probably also be an error to suppose that a person who goes from the one kind of faith to the other must now understand both because he has really experienced both. Rather, it is to be suspected that a philosopher who comes to religious faith was never engaged in authentic philosophizing. What happens to a religious believer who comes to philosophize, however, is perhaps a matter of the tension within that faith itself.

The consequences of this insight is that within the philosophical viewpoint a position develops which seems paradoxical when measured by the thought of a single universally valid truth:

a) Philosophy must come to grips with the claims made by *truth outside philosophy itself.* It is concerned with what it can never itself become and without which it yet would not be what it is. How it is related to religion, to the reality apprehended in religion, and to the reality of religious believers are basic questions for a living philosophy which have no final answers.

b) Between philosophy and religion there is a *conflict.* As long as it is a conflict over truth rather than worldly existence, and is conducted in a spirit of reasons, facts, and questions rather than by force, the following rule holds: whenever philosophy and religion are compared to each other, both must be envisioned on the same level, not one in an exalted and the other in a degenerate form.

A *philosophy* whose advocate lacks faith because he lacks Existenz, thus falling into empty thinking and specious assertion, slipping into mere immanence, and becoming entangled in a claim to absolute knowledge, is no more a philosophy than a *religion* that fixes upon the mindless representation of an alleged supersensible object remains religion. When this happens, the fight against the barrenness, disintegrating effects and frivolous character of philosophy is as justified as the fight against the fanaticizing and destructive consequences of superstition in religion, and against the lack of Existenz in its advocates.

Completely different from animosity toward religion, however, is the essentially alien character of religion to philosophy. Philosophical thinking makes us aware of a source which finds no satisfactory expression in religious form. This source receives a fulfillment as philosophy awakens us to the perception of—rather than simply giving us—reality. This reality comes forth as uncomprehended as does religious reality. It is that which sustains everything in the philosophizing person and his world.

In its remoteness from religion, however, philosophy *cannot attack as false* a religion that remains true to its own source. In philosophizing, we recognize religion as true in a way we do not understand, recognize it in a continuing readiness and questioning will to understand. To be constantly perplexed anew by religion belongs to the very life of philosophy. The relationship between philosophy and religion is a conflict which, by its nature, ceases to be carried on by philosophy when it reaches that decisive point which does not comprehend. In philosophizing we affirm the existence of ecclesiastical religion as the sole form of the substantial tradition to which the tradition of philosophy, too, is bound. We may become absorbed with philosophy in the tension of religious reality, not, however, as a foundation, but as the pole without which even religion seems to us to disappear.

Thus wherever general assertions and demands claiming validity in the world for everyone are made from the viewpoint of religion, we enter the common medium of question and verification, and are engaged in a never-ending conflict.

c) In this, philosophy presupposes that its thought, which seems to endanger religion, cannot in fact be a threat to a true religion. Whatever does not stand up to thought cannot be genuine; nor can that which refuses to listen and be questioned. Unrelenting thought will cause whatever possesses an authentic origin to arise all the more purely and clearly. Degenerate religion, however, is justifiably exposed to the danger of attack.

The third question:

The history of the last few centuries seems to point an urgent lesson: the loss of religion changes everything. It destroys both authority and exception. Everything seems doubtful and fragile. Nothing unconditioned remains when the conclusion is drawn that nothing is true, everything is permitted. Along with the perplexity resulting from being unable to find a firm ground, a narrow, confining and unthinking fanaticism arises. If religion as the presence of transcendence vanishes, so does authentic reality. Religion has become powerless. It is like an externally glittering but internally decayed figure—one push and it crumbles without resistance into dust, mysteriously taking down with it the one who pushes.

All forces that threaten religion are then considered ruinous for mankind generally. Among them philosophy and the sciences seem to be included. Because of the popularization of philosophy in recent times, a quantity of empty "enlightenment" thoughts adding up to an intellectual dogma has become everyone's common property. As everyone has come to share in the sciences, a superstitious belief in poorly understood scientific doctrines has become pervasive.

During this same time a loss of consciousness of humanity has occurred, particularly an irresistible submersion even of the ability to understand and appreciate human capacities, human destinies and surging aspirations, which up to the nineteenth century had their expression in poetry and their reality in living men. When Homer, Sophocles, Dante, Shakespeare, and Goethe mean progressively less to people, one hears the accusation that science and philosophy are to blame. Have they not taught people to doubt everything in superficial thinking? Have they not blocked off the depths as a consequence of their rationalism? Reality now is nothing but what can be known about it by natural knowledge—that is, in the end, a banal facticity.

The question is whether philosophy ought not to be rejected as a ruinous and disintegrative way of thinking.

In *answer* one must say that such general, accusing assertions about causal connections are questionable. They are suggestive, but do not bear up under scrutiny. We have had too much of these—pessimistic or optimistic—sweeping judgments about world-history and the future. To be sure, we want to know the possibilities and trace out the vast unknown; but first of all we want here and now to do and be what we can, and what is to be realized now—and what does not depend upon world-historical total knowledge.

In this matter the task of *philosophizing* is and remains to open us up—to the breadth of the encompassing, the daring to communicate in every sense of truth in a loving struggle, ever patiently preserving reason alert even in the presence of both what is most foreign and of what withdraws in failure, and ultimately to find the way home to reality. Is this task possible?

There is an ancient saying that in the sciences a little knowledge leads away from faith, but that complete knowledge leads back to it. Indeed, to know something scientifically means to know it critically and methodically, to know what one knows and what he does not know. It means to be aware of the limits of knowledge and to bring a philosophical spirit to science. Without this spirit the propositions and words expressing scientific results are superstitions.

We can apply the saying about the sciences to philosophy: a little philosophy leads away from reality, but complete philosophy leads back to it. Superficial philosophy may well have the consequences which the accusing vision of the present age ascribes to it. It may fritter itself away in endless problems, in historical knowledge of school doctrines, in bright ideas, in see-sawing intellectual deliberations—and lose reality in the process. Complete philosophy, however, is master of these possibilities. It is essentially the concentration whereby man becomes himself by sharing in reality.

Although complete philosophy can stir every man, indeed even children, in the form of simple but effective thoughts, its conscious elaboration is a never ending task which must ever be repeated, but which nevertheless is constantly accomplished as a present totality. The consciousness of this task, in whatever form it appears, will remain keen as long as men remain men. Perhaps only a few will ever really follow it. But it is a noble way: "All noble things are as difficult as they are rare."

Epilogue

At the request of the publisher, I am re-issuing these lectures of 1937, which have long been un-available, even though most of the ideas in them are contained in my long book, *Von der Wahrheit,* from whose manuscript they were taken at the time. The new printing permits me to say something about the meaning of "Existenz" in the situation from which these lectures sprang.

The expression "philosophy of existence" has a history that is not wholly transparent. As far as I am aware it was first publicly used by Fritz Heinemann in his *Neue Wege der Philosophie* (1929); and he makes a claim to priority.[1] By an anonymous process over the years since then, it has come to be a catch-word for contemporary philosophizing. Heinemann's use of the word at that time did not strike me as strange, for I have been using it in my lectures since the middle twenties and, because of Kierkegaard, did not suspect it of being anything new. It was not my intention to teach a new philosophy by using it, nor did I think that I was doing so. In my lectures

1. *Heinemann makes this claim in* Existentialism and the Human Predicament *(Harper Torchbooks, 1958), p. 1. (Tr.)*

I used the phrase "elucidation of Existenz" for one part of philosophy. I thus did not take Heinemann's book as in effect creating a new modern philosophy by giving it a name. But Heinemann carried the day as far as public usage is concerned. The word *Existenzphilosophie* (especially in referring to Heidegger as the originator of *Existentialphilosophie*) was seized upon to stigmatize contemporary philosophizing in so far as it is not logistical and traditional; and it is now ineradicable. Although all the authors who are considered its inaugurators have repudiated it, it remains like a phantom under whose name the most heterogeneous things are treated as identical. In my *Man in the Modern Age* (1931), I used this word for a philosophical way of thinking about man. My *Philosophy*, published at the same time, dealt with the elucidation of Existenz in only one of its three volumes. I also spoke of "the philosophy of existence," in the sense of these lectures, according to which "for the moment Existenz is the key word" of philosophy. Although I accepted the word as the title of these lectures, I wanted to avoid the catch-word. At that time it was not yet misleading. Sartre's existentialism, which has conquered the world, did not yet exist. This has sprung from an alien philosophical frame of mind. It was still possible to designate something entirely different with the word.

This something different was the only thing I had in mind. The lectures were written in the weeks following my dismissal from my professorship (because my wife is Jewish, not on account of my unknown political views or because my philosophy was of no interest). In the person of its director, Prof. Ernst Beutler, the academy held to its previously issued invitation despite my dismissal. I knew that I would not again be able to speak out publicly. I seized upon this last opportunity and regarded it as an unexpected stroke of fortune that, thanks to the publisher, these lectures could even be published. They were my last publication until the destruction of National Socialism made free German life possible again in the West. Their mood bespeaks of moment in which they came into being—it refers to the indestructible.

What was I to say? Symbolically, in the days of these lectures, I was more than normally weakened by a physical illness; I raised an almost hopeless voice in that moment. This voice was to recall. It moved in philosophy, from whence, far rational beings, comes everything having validity, strength and foundation when ecclesiastical-religious faith does not give support.

But I made no direct allusions to what the National Socialists were doing. That would have been fatal at the time. I was one of those who were resolved not to fall prey to the terror apparatus through carelessness. For not only did the state of my personal vitality make me unfit for concerted and active resistance, but as a lone professor I very likely would not have decided to act even if circumstances had favored it. To me there seemed nothing left beyond at least being at all times clear about what I was doing and intending to do, and to act accordingly. What we had to do was to act naively, to pretend no interest in the affairs of the world, to preserve a natural dignity (which still protected us in many situations), and if need be to lie without scruples. For beasts in possession of an absolute power to destroy must be treated with cunning and not as men and rational beings. Spinoza's "avoidance,"[2] a high and hard demand, was

2. *"Caute." Jaspers must be referring to Spinoza's "Cautio" developed in the proof of Prop. 59, Bk. IV of the* Ethics, *where he says: ". . . an equally great virtue or fortitude of mind is required to restrain daring as to restrain fear, that is, a free man declines dangers with the same mental virtue as that with which he attempts to overcome them." (Tr.)*

continually before our eyes; yet to follow that demand was not enough. I have dealt with the hazards of this situation in my book, *Die Schuldfrage* (1946, transl. as *The Question of German Guilt*, 1947) and will not repeat myself here.

Our personal situation was a reflection of the German calamity. The mood was set by our knowledge of the destruction of the German soul and spirit that was in progress. Since 1934, the phrase "finis Germaniae" circulated in our Heidelberg circle. At that time none of us suspected what was to come. In comparison with the later monstrosities, the relatively small ones of 1937 pale into insignificance. The rescue of the possibilities of German life through the annihilation of National Socialism by foreign forces still lay beyond the horizon.

There was a small circle of friends who spoke openly and without reservations among themselves, with complete confidence in one another's trustworthiness, and with a common caution. To me personally, as to them, the only possibility that remained was the hidden life of thought where we could establish an alibi for the German essence at least in spirit. I became German in a way I had never been conscious of, not in a national but an ethical sense. Believing in my own German essence, I defied the progressively more horrible, depraved and inhuman environment, in which one could only be silent if he wanted to survive.

In these lectures, I said what could be said without risk: only philosophy. This was still possible because the National Socialists, from the highest leaders down to the most insignificant functionaries, in spite of their surpassing intelligence in organization, techniques, propaganda and sophistry, were unbelievably stupid (in contrast to the Russian communists) in respect of things of the mind.

Besides, they were contemptuous of philosophy which, according to them, no one could understand anyway.

What I said in these lectures was not meant just for the moment, though it was formulated in the hopelessness of that moment. The development of these thoughts shows something of this background. I was encouraged later on when I occasionally heard that men who were strangers to me experienced "consolation" in reading this book, such as philosophy can give by the claim it makes on us.

Under this total threat, I paid homage to reason, to the commitment to the sciences, to the search for what is essential, and to the thinking that goes to the ground of all being—but the content as such was so little determined by the historical situation that I cannot find one sentence in it which I would consider timebound and therefore obsolete. Where one speaks of the encompassing, of truth, and of reality, what he says is valid even in the absence of the extreme distress in which it was thought out.

KARL JASPERS

Basel, May, 1956